AKZO NOBEL
INDUSTRIAL COATINGS LTD

COATING WITH CONFIDENCE

www.akzonobel-ic.co.uk

Akzo Nobel Industrial Coatings Ltd
PO Box 37, Crown House, Hollins Road,
Darwen, Lancashire, England, BB3 0BG
Tel: 01254 760760 Fax: 01254 701692

Darwen Football Club
Memories

By Paul Breeze

First Published in Great Britain
July 2001
By

Posh Up North Publishing, 3 Hunter Street
Nelson, Lancashire, BB9 5JG

British Library Catolguing-in-Publication Data
A catalogue record for this book is available from
the British Library

ISBN: 0-9539782-4-9

Printed by:
ProPrint
Riverside Cottage
Great North Road
Stibbington
Peterborough PE8 6LR

Front cover: Darwen FC v Rochdale Reserves - Early 1930s
Source: Blackburn with Darwen Library & Information Service

Back cover: Darwen FC team photo at Barley Bank mid 1899
Source: Marjorie Bibby

Messages of Support

" ...Mr Wenger would like to wish you every success with your proposed book and send Darwen FC very best wishes for the future from everyone at Arsenal"

Arsenal Football Club, May 2001

Acknowledgements

I would like to thank the following for their help in the preparation of this book:

DFC Chairman Kath Marah for her continued support and backup
Ex-DFC secretary Jack Howarth for allowing me access to his notes.

My "interviewees": Bert Proos, Marjorie Bibby, Nora Thompson, Jack Robinson, Bob Eccles, Ron Parry, Jimmy Birkett, Jimmy Khan, Steve Wilkes, Steve Hart, Brian Isherwood, Norman Walsh, Mick Higgins, Vic the gateman.

The staff at Darwen & Blackburn Libraries
Dave Twydell, Yore Publications
Stewart Fells, Radcliffe
Ken Ormerod, Morecambe
David Howgate, Southport
Slater Family
Hamilton Family, Australia
Mrs B Merrick
Amy Bassnet & Annie Holden
One Stop Copy Shop, Darwen
Lancashire Evening Telegraph
Non League Paper
Association for Football Statisticians
Richard Rundle - The Football Club History Database
(http://www.fchd.btinternet.co.uk/)

And of course, my partner Deirdre for her support in proof reading, brainstorming, telephoning and generally putting up with me while all this has been going on.

Contents

Introduction

This book does not set out to be a "complete record" of Darwen Football Club.

The club has fallen victim to several fires in recent years and has lost most of its early archives. As such the information used here has come from a variety of sources and therefore does not offer the uniformity of detail and content that I might otherwise have liked.

Rather than a tedious amble through over 130 years of facts and figures, this book aims to concentrate on the triumphs of the Darwen club during its long history and focuses mainly on the successful teams and the top players of any given period.

Wherever it has been possible, I have preferred to use first hand accounts and personal memories, rather than just rattle off lists of statistics, although this does serve to make the book appear a little imbalanced in certain sections.

I only became acquainted with Darwen Football Club quite recently – on the occasion of their ATS Trophy final appearance against Morecambe in April 1999 – and was so impressed with the way that they took a team from 4 divisions higher than them all the way to penalties that I felt I had to find out more.

The early history of the club, its FA Cup exploits, the early use of professional players and its brief period in the Football League has made very interesting research material for me and I hope the account given here reflects my enthusiasm for the subject.

Chapter One: Pre-League

Early History

Football, of a sort, has been played in and around Darwen since the late 1700s. However, the game played at that time was more of the "Shrove Tuesday mass brawl" variety than anything like the "soccer" that we know today. There were very few rules, and play was often quite brutal.

In the 1820s, the Darwen team were unbeatable in their district but, as play became more and more violent (in 1829 hammers and cleavers were used as weapons on the field of play), this style of game eventually began to peter out.

Francis Brindle, an ex soldier who had fought against Napoleon Bonaparte, commented upon a famous match on 17th May 1830 between Tottington and Darwen: *"nothing at Waterloo was half as bad as what I've seen this afternoon."*

Modern day football as we know it today originated in the public schools of the mid 1800s and Nathaniel Walsh, owner of the Orchard Mill in Darwen, sent his sons to Harrow, which was one of the game's leading establishments. During the school holidays, the boys introduced the game to the mill workers and everything took off from there with teams quickly being formed around the local factories.

According to a retrospective article written in the *Northern Daily Telegraph* in 1931, the first "proper" football match to be played in Darwen occurred in 1872 when the Orchard Mill team played against the Union Street Mill team. Following that game, a meeting was held at the watchhouse at Orchard Mill and the first Darwen Football Club was formed.

There are varied opinions as to how and when the first Darwen Football Club had been founded but, as, at the time that article was written, three surviving players from that first game were still alive - Peter Duckworth and Eli Kirkham of Orchard Mill and Moses Neville of Union Street Mill - it may be reasonably assumed that the account is correct.

For its first season of play, the club used a field at Lynwood - ironically, not far from the present Anchor Ground - where they played their first match, losing 1-3 to a team from Brookhouse.

Peter Duckworth
(Source: Northern Daily Telegraph 29.8.31)

For its second season, the club moved from its Lynwood ground to a new home at Barley Bank, a large ground where cricket was already being played. In its early years, the football club actually operated as part of the cricket club and was known as the Darwen Cricket and Football Club.

At this time, the Darwen club was playing to the London Football Association rules but then switched in 1874 to play the Rugby game for a couple of years in common with many of the other emerging teams in the north of England.

Darwen switched back to London Association rules for good in 1877 so that they would then be able to take part in the London Association's Challenge Cup - better known as the FA Cup. The Cup had been introduced in England in 1871 and had, up to then, only been played for by teams from the south - mainly public schools and other gentlemen's sporting clubs.

After this switch back to Association rules, the Darwen team quickly established themselves as one of the top teams in the area and, in 1878, became the first club from Lancashire to enter the FA Cup.

They won their first match over a Manchester team by 3 goals to nil and were then drawn against Sheffield. Several hundred spectators watched the match as Darwen lost to a single goal (marked down in the records as "disputed"...). Don't forget that, in those days, the idea of referee and linesmen as we know it had not been introduced - and such dispute-saving innovations as goal nets were not introduced until 1891

The other top team in the area was the neighbouring Turton club who had not lost a home game for seven years. When the Darwen team played an away match there, the game aroused such interest that a special train was laid on to allow 1,000 Darwen fans to travel to the match. The "Darreners" came away with a shock 1-0 win to reinforce Darwen's reputation as the top team in the north west.

A typical goalmouth scrimmage of the 1880s
(source: Yore Publications)

5

First Professional Players

On 1st January 1878, Darwen played host to Scottish side Partick in a friendly match that was a watched by some 3,000 people. In the Partick team that day were two players - Fergus Suter and James Love - who both, apparently, liked the town of Darwen so much that they decided they would like to move there and play for the Darwen team.

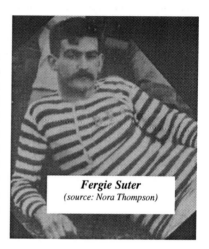

Fergie Suter
(source: Nora Thompson)

Suter was a stonemason by trade and he wrote to advise the club that he was planning to take up work nearby.

As Association Football had originated in the south of England and was played by purely amateur clubs, the idea of paid professional players posed a real threat to the amateur nature of the game in England. The arrival in Darwen of not just Suter but also Love and one of Suter's relatives who happened to be a goalkeeper of some repute raised for the first time question marks over the club's amateur status.

Darwen club chairman Mr Thomas Hindle denied that the newly arrived players were being paid by the club but, as Suter was never seen actually doing any stonemasonry (he said that the local stone was harder to work on than the Scottish variety…), it was difficult to see how else he might be earning his living. As such it is thought that he and Love were, in fact, the world's first paid professional football players

Harry Kay, news editor of the *Northern Daily Telegraph* in the 1940s, explains this early form of illegal professionalism: *"Clubs used to go to a tremendous lot of trouble (and expense) to make guest players from Scotland as comfortable as possible. So much did Scots appreciate this consideration that they forgot all about their work...and lived on kind words and fresh air."*

The arrival of these supposed paid professionals brought complaints from the other Lancashire clubs but, at that time, the FA didn't even have a rule on its books to govern such an eventuality and little, in practice, could be done about it.

Rules on professionalism were later introduced by the FA but were flouted so openly by the clubs in the north of England that the top level of football in England gradually lost its amateur status altogether. The practice was finally legalised in England in 1885 after some Lancashire clubs got together and threatened to form their own "British Football Association". By the time the Football League was founded in 1888, all the member clubs were fully professional and all came from the north of England or the Midlands.

Suter eventually left Darwen in the summer of 1880 and went to play for Blackburn Rovers. With them, he won 3 FA Cup winners medals but fell foul of the Scottish FA's policy of not picking players who played in England (professionalism was not legalised in Scotland until 1892), otherwise he would undoubtedly have won many international caps.

James Love was not so lucky and, according to Darwen historian Howard Peters, was killed in the bombardment of Alexandria, Egypt in 1882, although no mention is made of when and how he made the transition from soccer star to Royal Navy combatant.

Lancashire Football Association

On 28th September 1878, the LFA was officially formed at a meeting at the Co-operative Hall in Darwen and Darwen's Thomas Hindle became the first chairman.

The new Association had been the brainchild of Hindle and Blackburn Rovers chairman John Lewis and initially consisted of 28 member clubs. It is interesting to note that, in those early days, these founder members were not widely spread across Lancashire. In fact, all 28 clubs came from the 6 neighbouring towns of Blackburn, Bolton, Church, Darwen, Haslingden and Rawtenstall as rugby football was still prevalent elsewhere in the county.

Hindle occupied the post of chairman until 1882 at which time he was offered the post of honorary treasurer - a function he fulfilled until 1919.

Lancashire County Matches

On 16th December 1878, the Barley Bank ground hosted the first ever Lancashire team trial at which six players from Darwen were selected to represent the county in forthcoming matches.

On 4th January 1879, the Lancashire FA played its first representative game - against North Wales. As with the earlier trial match, this game was also staged at Barley Bank and four Darwen players - Suter, Moorhouse, Gledhill and Bury - were present in the eleven that drew 1-1 with the Welsh.

In the return game on 15th February at Wrexham Racecourse, Marshall replaced Moorhouse in the line up as Lancashire won 2-1 with Darwen's Bury scoring one of the goals.

In the months that followed, the Darwen club's dominance over football in the North West was further reflected in the Lancashire team selections. 5 players from Darwen were present in the team that won 2-1 away to Cheshire on 29th March: Moorhouse, Bury (1g), R Kirkham, Gledhill, Marshall (1g). Marshall and Rostron went on to become almost permanent fixtures in the representative XI.

The following season, when Lancashire beat North Wales 4-2 at Turton, there were no fewer than 6 Darwen players in the team. - Suter, Fish, Marshall, Rostron, Gledhill, Bury (2g), R Kirkham (1g) - a fact that provoked complaints from the other leading Lancashire clubs that the selectors were biased.

Darwen's W Marsden wearing an example of a Lancashire county cap for the 1889/90 season
(source: Blackburn with Darwen Library & Information Service)

First Floodlit Football Match

On 28th October 1878 Darwen entertained a composite team from Blackburn at the Barley Bank ground in one of the first ever floodlit matches to be held in the country.

Several thousand spectators were present to watch this unusual spectacle and were thrilled to see Darwen beat their opponents by 3 goals to nil.

The *Darwen News* of 7th November described the match. The first section of the report is reproduced below, however, it went on for a further 3 columns of text, writing much more about the technology of the lighting than about the actual game!

GRAND

FOOTBALL MATCH
BY THE
ELECTRIC LIGHT.

From every point of view, the football match played at Darwen, on Thursday evening, by aid of the electric light, was a brilliant success. The spectators assembled in thousands; the light was truly marvellous to behold; the play of the football teams was thoroughly spirited, and the novel proceedings passed off without a single hitch of any note whatever. Considerable interest was manifested in the contest between the Darwen and Blackburn teams, but, as it was only natural to expect, the football match was only of secondary interest to the wonderful electric light by the aid of whose illumination it was played.

The electric light as an illuminator of large areas is as great an improvement upon gas as was gas itself upon the antiquated tallow candle. Though sparklingly brilliant, paling the brightness of the stars in the dark firmament above, the electric light was soft and mild, quite pleasant to look upon, giving no pain or inconvenience to the eye by long gazing at its brilliance, at any rate to those onlooking from a distance, and it was clear, constant, steady, and without blemish. It was incomparably superior to the dim-yellow gas lights in the town which were visible from the football grounds and the heights above; indeed so strong was its illuminating powers that, with a little difficulty, we could read ordinary newspaper type and manuscript by its light, when standing on Tookholes-road, which our readers know is a considerable distance from the field in which the electric lights were situate, whilst it was quite an easy matter to tell the time by one's watch or to recognise acquaintances at the same distance. We must in candour admit hearing several people complain that the electric light did not approach their expectation, but if it really did not what in the world had their extraordinary imaginations led them to expect? Not a chained comet, surely!

1879 - Early FA Cup Glory

In the 1878/79 season's FA Cup, Darwen were awarded a bye in the first round after the Birch club from Manchester withdrew and, in the second round, they were drawn against the Eagley club. This encounter was much anticipated after a 2-2 friendly draw between the two clubs at Darwen at the end of the previous season.

As it turned out, the match was quite memorable but for the wrong reason. Dr J Gledhill, a Darwen player based in Manchester, got off his train at the wrong station and missed the game! In those days teams did not have large playing squads and substitutes so Darwen had to play the match with ten men.

Despite being a man short, the match ended in a 0-0 draw and, this being in the days before replays at the opposing ground were mandatory, Darwen had to travel to Eagley again for the replay on 23rd December. Here again, they must have had transport problems as the game kicked off half an hour late but Darwen took the early initiative and cruised to a 4-0 lead by half time with Love scoring a hat-trick.

The final score of 4-1 put Darwen through to the next round of the cup where they were drawn against a top amateur club from Buckinghamshire - ex public schoolboys the Remnants.

The game was to be played at the Oval in London on 30th January 1879. It was a Thursday afternoon and this posed a problem to the Darwen team who were - with the obvious exception of Suter and Love - amateur players and, for the most part, full time cotton millworkers.

Despite good performances on the pitch, the club was not rich by any means and could not afford to pay for the trip down to London. Collections were made at matches prior to the trip and a benefit concert was held in Darwen in an attempt to raise the necessary funds.

One way or another, the money was scraped together and the Darwen team were able to take their place on the rather snow covered pitch at the Oval. The Darwen team that day was: Duxbury, Suter, Brindle, Moorhouse, Knowles, Marshall, Love, Gledhill, W Kirkham, Bury and R Kirkham.

The Remnants took an early lead but, instead of buckling, Darwen fought back and were level by half time. It was a similar story in the second half and a late equaliser for the millworkers took the match into extra time.

Most people had written off Darwen's chances even before the match had begun so this was already a moral victory for the Lancashire side. As extra time ticked by, the Remnants began to lose heart and, when Love scored to put Darwen ahead for the first time in the tie, a shock looked on the cards!

The score remained 2-3 as the final whistle blew and Darwen had notched up what could probably be considered one of the earliest examples of FA Cup giant killing!

The prize for this momentous victory was an even harder challenge in the next round - a tie against the Old Etonians who had appeared in the Cup final twice before and who had an awesome reputation. Unfortunately, the rules of he FA Cup in those days stated that all matches in the later rounds in the competition had to be played at the Oval reflecting the southern bias of the competition at that time. For Darwen, this meant another costly trip to London - one they could ill afford.

However, more collections were organised around the town and among local workers and individual contributions were also made by the mayor, town councillors and local tradesmen. Thus, with the generous backing of the townspeople, Darwen FC managed to get down to London again for the match on 13th February.

Once again tired from their journey, Darwen struggled to match the superior Old Etonians and, by half time, they were trailing 4-0.

As the second half began, the Old Etonians scored again and the game looked to be well beyond the reach of the Darreners. They did manage to pull a goal back as the Etonians appeared to ease off a little but, with 15 minutes left to play, the score remained 5-1.

Then, a little piece of luck came their way in the shape of an Old Etonians own goal! Love then dashed up the pitch to head a third for Darwen and, miraculously, a fourth goal quickly followed after mad scramble in front of the Old Etonians's goal. The referee disallowed this goal but, after appeals from the Darwen players, decided to let it stand.

And Darwen still had more to offer. Encouraged by their great second half fight-back, they carried on with the pressure and Love scored again just before the end of normal time to snatch a dramatic 5-5 draw!

In those early days of the FA Cup, it was not obligatory for extra time to be played in the event of a drawn game, although it was permissible if both teams agreed. Not surprisingly, Darwen were keen to play extra time but the Old Etonians were not.

The only other solution was a replay. Darwen mindful of the economics of yet another trip to London tried to persuade the Old Etonians to play the return game in Darwen - after all, the Oval was essentially their home ground. They even offered to pay for the Old Boys' travelling expenses up to Lancashire out of the £40 surplus they had made from their fund raising for this trip. But the Old Etonians, possibly wary of being beaten a bunch of mill-workers and, also quite probably, very disapproving of the professional nature of some of their players, refused.

The tie would have to, once again, be played at the Oval and, once again, the town of Darwen began feverish fundraising. This time they raised £ 175 for their third trek south. The Old Etonians themselves chipped in £5 and the FA, whose rules meant that the game had to be played again in London, also contributed £10.

Darwen found themselves back at the Oval for the third time in little over a month as, on 8th March, they faced the old boys in the replay. With a great display of skill, the Old Etonians took the lead but Darwen responded through R Kirkham for a half time score of 1-1.

The second half was played out in a similar fashion with the old boys once again taking the lead and Darwen once again scoring an equaliser. At the end of normal time it was 2-2 and 30 minutes' extra time also failed to produce another goal.

This result meant that a **third** match would have to be played in an attempt to separate the two teams. Again Darwen asked for the Old Etonians to travel up to Darwen. Again, they politely refused and pointed out - quite correctly - the fact that the FA rules required the all such later stage games to be played at the Oval.

Public sympathy right across the country was expressed in favour of Darwen's plight. It was clear that the FA Cup in its present format favoured southern-based teams too much and, in the season following the Darwen fiasco, the early rounds of the FA Cup were regionalised. This led to more teams from the North and the Midlands taking part.

By the time the third match was played, the Old Etonians had got used to Darwen's style of play - a more passing-based game, as played in Scotland - and had adopted some of their tactics in order to overcome them. By this time, the Darwen players who were, of course, still expected to work full time in between matches were feeling the strain of these long trips down to London and, not surprisingly, the Old Etonians won on this occasion 6-2.

This period saw the Darwen club at its best with regular victories over its local rivals. Between 1878 and 1881 they took many notable scalps including: Preston North End (14-1), Blackburn Association (11-0), Blackburn Olympic (8-2), Liverpool (13-0), Partick (4-1), and Turton (5-2 away).

The *East Lancs Cricket and Football Times* commented: *"the club's record surely cannot be equalled by any other club in the Palatine"*.

The Lancashire Cup

Before the Football League was introduced, there was not much serious competition and, once a club was knocked out of the FA Cup, they had little to offer their spectators than friendly games against mixed levels of opposition. In order to maintain the interest of the fans and, indeed, the players, the Lancashire FA decided to set up its own county cup competition.

The beautifully ornate cup stood 3ft 3in high and cost £160.00 to purchase. In its early days, the Lancashire Cup was highly prized and was the cause of numerous rifts between Darwen and Blackburn Rovers.

The new cup competition became so popular that a secondary competition - the Lancashire Junior Cup - had to be introduced in 1885 because too many clubs were trying to enter the main tournament. This Junior Cup gave smaller clubs a more realistic chance of winning a trophy and helped reduced the number of one-sided games in the Senior Cup.

However, once national league competition took over as the main focus for serious football, a greater gulf soon appeared between the professionals in the League and the amateurs in the other teams and these county-based tournaments began to lose their appeal.

This was compounded by the fact that the League clubs would often scratch or send a weakened team to take on their lesser light opponents. The situation developed to such an extent that, after the First World War, the Lancashire Cup was restricted to include only Lancashire clubs that were playing in the Football League, with the remaining clubs playing for the LFA Junior Cup instead.

There came a brief u-turn in the 1930s when interest in the Senior Cup among the Football League clubs was so low that the leading junior clubs such as Darwen were, once again, invited to take part. The plan was to inject new interest and try and revive the flagging tournament. It didn't work and the Lancashire Senior Cup was later discontinued altogether.

It was resurrected in 1982 as a pre-season friendly tournament sponsored by the Isle of Man Tourism Dept under the guise of the "Lancashire Manx Cup".

In stark contrast, the Junior Cup was a great success and continues to be so to this day. It has now attracted sponsorship and has recently been known as the ATS Trophy and the Marsden Trophy.

As will be discussed in greater detail later on, Darwen reached the final of the Lancashire Senior Cup three times in all, winning the first ever final 3-0 over Blackburn Rovers.

They met their local rivals again in the final in 1882 but lost 3-2 and, after that, the Darwen club had to wait until the early 1890s to experience any sort of success in the competition.

Darwen FC 1879-80
Back: Duxbury, Fish, Brindle, Broughton, Moorhouse
Middle: Marshall, Rostron, Dr Gledhill, Holden, Kirkham, Bury
Front: Suter

(source: Nora Thompson)

Local Rivalries

Being so closely situated, there has always been rivalry between Darwen and Blackburn Rovers. In the 1870s, Darwen clearly had the upper hand and, in the early 1880s, the rivalry was close and fierce but since the formation of the Football League, Blackburn have had the better fortunes.

One of the first recorded "bouts" of contention between the two neighbouring clubs came in a match at Barley Bank on 12th April 1879.

Blackburn were leading 2-1 when Darwen were awarded a long throw close to the Rovers' goal. When the ball was thrown in, Rovers' McIntyre hoofed the ball so far out of the ground that much playing time was lost while attempts were made to recover it in a neighbouring field. (this was in the days before added time for stoppages and, seemingly, clubs did not have an abundance of match balls at their disposal...).

On 8th November 1879 McIntyre was at the centre of controversy again when a good 5,000 crowd was present at Barley Bank to see the first match between the two clubs since the "time wasting incident".

This time McIntrye charged into Darwen's goalkeeper Duxbury who had just punched the ball clear. The press report from the time suggested that McIntyre *"in a most brutal and certainly a most unwarrantable ungentlemanlike and ungamelike manner had basely and foully charged him in a vital place"*.

Duxbury was knocked unconscious and was only able to play on after centre forward Dr Gledhill had treated him. He tried to carry on but, almost immediately, gave away an equalising goal. He collapsed again and was carried off. The match ended in a 1-1 draw.

Darwen played Blackburn in the cup a week or so later and Duxbury was not fit to play. Many Darwen fans saw this as the main reason that they lost the ensuing match.

20th March 1880 - Lancashire Cup Final.

Some 8,000 spectators - the biggest attendance for a football match in Lancashire at that time - were present at Darwen's Barley Bank ground.

Blackburn started off the better side but Darwen scored against the run of play. By the end of the game they had added two more unanswered goals for an easy 3-0 win. The third goal was disputed, as often happened in the early days of football - and still happens to day, in fact!

On this occasion, the two umpires (linesmen and referees as we know them today had not been introduced at that time) couldn't make up their minds. The referee - more of an overseer than a true "man in middle" - decided to give the goal, although he was not actually empowered to make such a decision under the FA rules at the time.

This was not the only FA rule that was breached on that afternoon. There was also a rule stating that players had to live within a certain distance of their club. The inference was that, if a player was not a local man, then he could not possibly be playing as an amateur as he would have no means of support in the town. He must, therefore, be playing as a paid professional.

Blackburn had a player - AN Hornby the famous all-round sportsman who had captained Lancashire at cricket and played international rugby - who didn't fulfil this criteria but nor did Darwen's Kirkham. The FA ruled that both teams could field their questionable player and, while Darwen took advantage of this leniency, Blackburn did not.

Blackburn were also annoyed that the Lancashire FA had ordered the final to be played at Darwen's home ground. The Rovers initially refused to play the match at all but eventually relented and left Hornby out of the team.

Two weeks later Darwen played away at Blackburn and, again, won by three goals to nil and this did nothing to calm the bad feeling that was, by now, growing between the two neighbouring clubs.

In the summer of 1880, Fergie Suter left Darwen for what were termed "personal reasons" - presumably monetary. In fact, he was soon to be found "working" in the notional role of a tape sizer at a cotton mill in Blackburn.

In line with the bizarre measures against professionalism at the time, this meant that he was now eligible to play for a Blackburn club and, not surprisingly, Suter was soon to be seen playing for Blackburn Rovers. This attracted wide criticism in the Darwen press, only serving to increase the continuing antagonism.

Everything finally came to a head on 27th November 1880 when Darwen travelled to Blackburn's Alexandra Meadows for a "friendly" game with the Rovers. This was to be the first match between the two local rivals since Fergie Suter's move to Blackburn and, as such, everybody had been talking about it for weeks beforehand.

Over 10,000 fans were present and were tightly packed into the ground. In fact, Mike Jackman in *"Blackburn Rovers - a Complete Record "* puts the crowd at nearer 15,000, but all accounts agree that there were far too many people than could be safely contained. The grandstand was full and 20 horse lorries were brought in with boards to provide extra seating.

In *"Olympic FC"*, Graham Phythian gives a particularly colourful account of the game, stating that the start was delayed due the unmanageable nature of the crowd with the police having to intervene in one section of the ground.

Towards the end of a fiercely contested first half and with the match still goalless, Darwen were awarded a corner. Tot Rostron quickly took the corner but, as the crowd were encroaching onto the pitch, he took the kick from a position some seven or eight yards in from the corner flag.

Kirkham was the first to the ball for Darwen and scored. The goal was allowed to stand and the Darwen fans cheered but the Rovers fans - incensed that it had come from an illegal corner kick - spilled onto the pitch. The game was held up for 7 minutes while police tried to clear them off. Blackburn equalised before halftime and this caused another pitch invasion.

After 8 minutes of the second half, an incident occurred between Fergie Suter and Darwen's England international Thomas Marshall. Marshall received the ball and was running down the wing past a crush of Blackburn supporters when Suter knocked him off balance with a heavy charge. Marshall fell but got up quickly and grabbed Suter. As the pair pushed and shoved each other - each trying to knock the other over - they both fell to ground near the touchline.

Because the barriers had already been damaged in the earlier pitch invasions, some members of the crowd were able to get onto the pitch again and joined in with the ensuing brawl.

A mass pitch invasion then broke out from several sides of the ground at once and, this time, the police were unable to do anything about it. Members of the press were pelted with mud by the brawling fans and the game had to be abandoned. When the Darwen players finally managed to leave the field, they found that their dressing room had also been vandalised.

The fight gave rise to the following verse, which may go some way to explaining the reasoning behind it:

> *"Aw see thad Suter-Marshall scrap*
> *A yarra brief and bloodless mill*
> *An aw'm quite sure as nayther chap*
> *Bore t'other player t'least ill will*
> *Yo'see eawr Darren friends were cute*
> *But t' Rovers proved a trifle cuter*
> *An' t' gradley cause o' t' whul dispute*
> *Were t' Rovers nobblin' Mac an' Suter"*

("Tum O'Dick O'Bobs", 1880)

The return friendly match, which had been planned for later in the season, was called off by Blackburn and the animosity between the two clubs continued unabated.

In the new year, both clubs were hauled in front of the Lancashire FA to explain the incident. Marshall apologised, stating that *"no blows were struck"* but Suter did not apologise.

Darwen and Blackburn were due to play each other again in the Lancashire Cup and the bad feeling that had been brewing since the previous meeting - not helped by the local newspapers in both towns whipping up animosity - was set to continue. Darwen said that they would not meet the Rovers in the cup until they agreed to play the cancelled friendly match.

Blackburn eventually agreed to restage the friendly after the Lancashire Cup tie, which was supposed to have been played on 5th March 1881.

However Darwen had FA Cup commitments that day, having beaten Sheffield Wednesday in the 4th round, they had been drawn to play Romford in the quarter final (see later this chapter). Blackburn then claimed a bye, citing the Lancs FA own cup rules but this was overruled and the two teams were ordered to play the tie a week later on 12th March.

Blackburn cancelled this rescheduled game at the last minute and played a lucrative friendly against Nottingham Forest instead. This, in turn, infuriated Darwen as they had originally been due to be playing Partick on that date - another lucrative match - and had cancelled it to allow the game with Blackburn to go ahead. In the end they had to arrange a friendly with nearby Accrington instead.

As the Lancashire Cup game had not been played, the Lancashire FA, threw both clubs out of the competition. Blackburn reacted by resigning, for a short while, from the Lancashire FA and by trying their best to sabotage the rest of the Cup competition by arranging high profile friendly matches to clash with the later rounds thus ensuring that their games were better attended.

Things were further complicated when, in November 1881, a year after the original incident, Darwen and Blackburn were drawn together in the FA Cup. Once again, Darwen refused to play Blackburn until the friendly game was restaged.

After a long drawn out consultation involving the English FA, it was agreed that the FA Cup tie would be played at Blackburn with the gate money divided equally between both clubs, after which the famous friendly would be played at Darwen. "The Big Match" - long awaited as it was - turned out to be a bit of a damp squib when it eventually took place on 18th March 1882 as Darwen lost 5-0.

***

There is another well-documented case of antagonism between Darwen and Blackburn but this did not take place until some 10 years after these earlier incidents. By 1890 Blackburn were a Football League side. They had gone unbeaten in their previous 6 League games when they arranged to play a friendly match against Darwen on Christmas Day 1890.

Blackburn were due to play Wolverhampton Wanderers away in a League match the next day and only fielded three or four first team players, presumably thinking that Darwen were, by then, easy opposition.

As admission prices had been increased at Ewood Park for this match, the crowd were not happy about this and the Darwen team took particular offence when they saw the composition of the Rover's side that took the field.

Egged on by an incensed Darwen away support, The Darreners' captain led his team off the pitch and, a few minutes later, the Darwen second team - who had presumably been in the crowd to watch the game - came out on to the field instead.

Now the Blackburn contingent of the crowd got annoyed as well and masses of spectators ran onto the pitch. The goal posts were torn out and the people in the press box were threatened and it was also reported that someone *"knocked the hat off a Rovers official...."*

The angry crowd only gave up and went home after police intervention and the offer of free tickets for another match.

***

In all fairness to Blackburn Rovers, it has to be pointed out that it was not just derby matches against the "old enemy" that were the cause of "rowdiness" among the crowd.

In 1886 Darwen travelled to Burnley with a weakened team. The hosts were at full strength - with many imported Scottish players - but, by half time, had only managed to build up a narrow 2-1 lead.

In the second half Darwen had the wind in their favour and, after much pressure, forced an equaliser. As Darwen pushed forward, Burnley broke away, shot for goal and claimed that the ball, caught by the Darreners' goalkeeper Holden, had crossed the line. The Darwen players denied this and argued profusely with both referee and umpires. During the confusion, a Burnley forward kicked off again from the centre spot and the ball ended up in the Darwen net.

The referee awarded the goal, which prompted the Darwen team to discuss leaving the field. At this point the Burnley crowd began throwing various missiles at the players. The Darwen players decided to play on (perhaps they thought it would be safer than trying to get off...) but were unable to score again.

The *Darwen News* of the time suggested that the Burnley crowd had expected their team to win by a much higher margin, as Darwen were only to field four first team players. The report states that, as the Darwen team left the field at the end they were *"pelted by stones and otherwise assaulted by the spectators in a disgraceful and cowardly manner."*

Darwen entertained Blackpool in a match played at the Barley Bank in 1890. It is not clear exactly what occurred but it is recorded that one Darwen player - Baker - was censured for swearing at the referee.

After the game, the Blackpool club complained that their players had been forced to leave the ground by climbing over a wall *"while being pelted with sods of earth and brickbats"*.

As a result of this, the referee in charge of the game was forced to resign from the Lancashire FA referees list and Darwen were ordered to post warning notices at the ground regarding future crowd conduct.

The Old Etonians and the FA Cup Trail Again

On New Year's Day 1880, the Old Etonians finally did the decent thing and came to Darwen for a friendly match as a mark of their respect for the team that had played so well against them in the 1878 FA Cup. On freezing cold morning, the old boys took to the field early to warm up but Darwen were the better side on the day and won the match 3-1.

After the game the Old Etonians were entertained at Orchard Bank, home of the mill-owning Walsh family, where James Walsh toasted his guests, observing that, as a Harrow boy, he *"seldom spoke well of Etonians"*.

In the FA Cup competition in the 1880 / 1881 season, Darwen put together a very impressive string of results

They followed up an 8-0 win over Brigg with an impressive 5-1 win away at Sheffield. Following a bye in 3rd round, they were drawn against another Sheffield side - the Wednesday club - who they easily beat 5-2 at home, Bury and Rostron were the goalscorers.

In the quarter-finals, Darwen were drawn away to Romford. However, quite possibly with one eye on the later rounds and the likelihood of yet more costly trips to the Oval, they managed to persuade them to switch the tie to Barley Bank and paid the Essex side to come up to Darwen instead. By half time the score was 11-0 and it finished 15-0 to Darwen - equalling the record score for the FA Cup at that time.

Darwen had reached the semi final of the FA Cup for the first time! This was the first time that any northern team had ever reached the semi final of the FA Cup. They were drawn against another public school old boys' team - Old Carthusians from Charterhouse - and had, once again, to play at the Oval.

Following their earlier exploits in the competition, Darwen were now most peoples' favorites to win the match and to become the first northern team to reach an FA Cup final. In store for them was the truly mouth watering prospect of a revenge match against the Old Etonians. "All" they had to do was to beat the Old Carthusians in the semi final first.

Darwen had the best of the early play and hit the post twice before taking a first half lead through Marshall. In the second half, it was a different story and the Carthusians fought back hard and, in the event, romped away 4-1 winners.

Away from cup games, Darwen's form began to slip in their friendly matches. On 8th January 1881 they lost 4-0 away at Aston Villa and followed this up with a 3-0 defeat away to Nottingham Forest.

Play Up Cards - early 1890s
(source: Yore Publications)

25

International Players

Away from local rivalries and battling to prove who had the best team locally, certain Darwen players gained wider recognition through their performances for club and county such that they were selected to play for England.

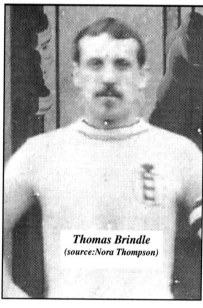

Thomas Brindle
(source:Nora Thompson)

One such player was Thomas Brindle who, in March 1880, became the first Darwen FC player to play for his country.

Having successfully negotiated his way through a North v South trial match at the Kennington Oval on 6th March, he made his international debut in a friendly game against Scotland, played in Glasgow on 13th March

He was the only player from the north of England in the team.

In his book *"An English Football Internationalists' Who's Who "* Douglas Lamming describes the left back as *"a powerful strong kicking back and a real work-horse"*.

The game ended in a 5-4 victory for the Scots but two days later England were victorious when they met Wales in Wrexham and beat them 3-2. Brindle not only played in this match but scored the winning goal as well!

Thomas Marshall
(source: Nora Thompson)

In Brindle's second international match he was joined by his Darwen team mate Thomas Marshall, who had also played in the North v South game. Marshall was born in Withnell, Lancs on 12th September 1858 and had been a professional sprinter before joining Darwen aged 20.

Lamming describes him as "*a fast winger, having the ability to pass the ball accurately when going full tilt*". His second and final cap came in a 1-0 defeat against Wales at Blackburn on 26th February 1881.

Thurston "Tot" Rostron was born in Darwen on 21st April 1863.

He played for several other local clubs before joining Darwen and made his England debut aged just 18 in the Wales match at Blackburn alongside Marshall.

His second England cap came when England lost 1-6 to Scotland at the Kennington Oval on 12th March 1881. Lamming describes him as a "*small but clever forward with plenty of pace, good screw kick and works hard*".

Tot Rostron
(source: Nora Thompson)

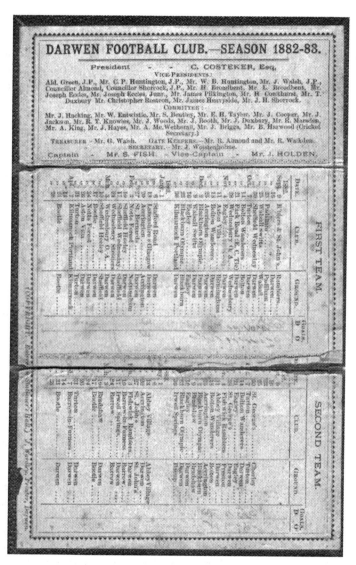

A Darwen FC fixture card for 1882/83
Opposition included Blackburn Olympic, Kilmarnock and Turton
(source: Nora Thompson)

1882 - East Lancashire Charity Cup

Following on from the warm reception accorded to the Lancashire Cup competition among competing clubs, another local cup competition - the East Lancashire Charity Cup - was brought into being.

In May 1882, representatives from Blackburn Rovers, Blackburn Olympic, Darwen and Accrington met at the White Bull Hotel in Blackburn and agreed to play a series of matches with the proceeds going to a good cause - the Blackburn and East Lancashire Infirmary.

According to Harry Kay, the cup was a magnificent trophy - 2ft 10 high, weighing 200 oz and cost almost £150 to have made: *"Engraved on the cup is a scene of the game of football and a picture of the infirmary. At the bottom are 4 figures of football players along with the crests of Blackburn, Darwen, Accrington and Burnley"*.

Each of the 4 clubs involved made a cash contribution towards the cost of the cup and also donated the gate receipts from the two semi finals and final. From the total £240 raised, £146/12s was spent on the cup, £8/15s/6d on its case £22 for medals for the winners and 2/15/0 on badges for the runners up. In the first final in 1882, Blackburn Olympic beat Blackburn Rovers 5-2.

The remaining balance of £40 was given as a charitable donation to the infirmary. Obviously, in the following years of the competition, the charitable donation was greater as the initial cost of the cup had already been met in the first season.

In the first two years of the East Lancs Charity Cup, Darwen met Blackburn Rovers in the semi final and lost on each occasion however, in 1884, they managed to reach the final for the first time, and won the cup by beating Accrington 1-0 after a replay. They won the cup twice more during their Lancashire League days (see Chapter Three) in 1901, beating Football League side Burnley 2-1 after two replays and again in 1902, beating Accrington Stanley 2-1.

Henry Hamilton

A member of the victorious Darwen team in 1884 was Henry Alexander Hamilton who, in his memoirs, described his playing time at Darwen thus:

"The Hibernian team then being in low water, I was welcomed into the ranks of the Darwen second eleven but I had only played with them a few matches when the Darwen committee thought me good enough for a place in their first team and in that place I played for 4 seasons.

The first season I played for the premier team I was rewarded with a medal from the Charity Cup committee, Darwen that year having won the cup.

I was persuaded at last to go to Stockton on Tees but only stayed a short time with them when Burnley wanted me and of course I went."

Henry Hamilton & his cup winner's Medal

Hamilton took over as Darwen captain following the departure of James Richmond. In the *Darwen News's* "Gallery of Football Notables", in 1886 it was stated that he *"fulfilled his post with great credit, having on several occasions refused tempting offers to play with other clubs,"* and *"stuck to his own club through thick and thin"*.

He also played one county game for Lancashire - on 6th February 1886 at Bootle. Lancashire beat Ulster 3-0 and Hamilton scored the 3rd goal. He gave up life as a football player in December 1890 when he joined the army where he played for his regimental team and went on to serve in the Boer War. He died in Chiswick, London in 1911 aged 44.

Chapter Two: Alliance and League

By the time the Football League was formed in 1888, Darwen had already begun to lose their status as one of the leading clubs in Lancashire - so much so that, in stark contrast to the start up of the Lancashire FA ten years beforehand, they were not even invited to the final discussions.

It was not so much that Darwen had got any worse, it was more a case of the rest of the North-West catching up with the Darreners and adopting many of the innovations that they had introduced.

With the legalisation of professionalism in England in 1885, there was no further advantage to be gained by illicitly using imported players. All clubs were now able to improve their playing staff openly and money became much more of a decisive factor than it had previously been. The bigger clubs with the bigger catchment areas could attract the better players and Darwen, in the immediate shadow of Blackburn and, to a certain extent, Accrington, gradually began to be edged out of the picture.

While other neighbouring teams such as Blackburn Rovers, Preston North End, Accrington, Bolton Wanderers and Burnley took over leading the way in football, and became founder members of the Football League in 1888, Darwen had to make do with joining the Football Alliance, which was a sort of next league down for teams that had failed to get through the ballot to join the big league.

The Alliance had been inspired by Nottingham Forest and Sheffield Wednesday who had also missed out on joining the league and played its first season of competition in 1889/90. Along with Darwen, they were joined in the new competition by Birmingham St Georges, Bootle, Crewe Alexandra, Grimsby Town, Long Eaton Rangers, Newton Heath, Small Heath (Birmingham), Sunderland Albion and Walsall Town Swifts.

ARDWICK (MAN CITY), BOOTLE, BURTON SWIFTS, CREWE ALEXANDRA, DARWEN, GRIMSBY, LINCOLN, NORTHWICH VICTORIA, PORT VALE, SHEFF UTD, SMALL HEATH (BIRMINGHAM CITY), WALSALL

(NEWTON HEATH, LIVERPOOL)

Looking forward to the new season, Darwen kicked off with a friendly fixture away at South Shore, drawing 2-2.

They played their first ever league game on 21st September 1889 at home to Birmingham St Georges. The team that day was: Holden, J Marsden, Leach, Thornber, Owen, T Marsden, Douglas, W Marsden, Fish, Smith & Entwistle but they made the worst possible start to their first ever league campaign losing by 7 goals to 3.

This was followed up by 3 more defeats on the trot - two away and one at home.

The run of poor form in the league was offset by cup wins - notably a 7-2 win away at South Shore in the Lancashire Cup and a 4-2 home win over Halliwell in the FA Cup but the Darwen public had to wait until 23rd November to see any success in the Football Alliance and it finally came with a 6-3 win over Walsall Town Swifts.

These mixed fortunes continued for much of the season. Having hammered South Shore in the Lancs Cup, Darwen then lost to them in the FA Cup but a 4-4 draw at Birmingham St Georges on Boxing Day signalled the start of an upswing.

Darwen then went the whole of January unbeaten in the league with 4 straight wins and did not lose another home game all season. They ended up 6th out of 12 in the final league table with a record of P 22 W10 D2 L10.

Having expected great things at the start of the campaign, this had turned out to be a fairly disappointing first season in league football. Darwen did not bother to apply for election to the Football League for season 1890/91, as had originally been the intention, and decided instead to remain in the Football Alliance for another year.

The following campaign did not turn out to be any more successful than the previous one and the club again finished in 6th position in the table with a record of P22, W10, D3 L9 and somewhat in debt.

Lancashire Cup Success Again

In the 1889/90 season, Darwen made good progress in the Lancashire Cup once again, reaching the semi finals. They were drawn against their old rivals, Blackburn Rovers, who were, by then, a top half side in the Football League but Darwen had home advantage as the tie was to be played at Barley Bank.

In the event, the game ended in a 1-1 draw and a replay was staged at Preston North End's Deepdale ground, which the Rovers won 2-0.

The following season, Darwen went one better and, beating Accrington, Burnley and Preston, reached the final where they were paired up with Bolton Wanderers, another comfortably placed Football League side. The match was played at Everton and Darwen were unlucky to lose 3-1 to a Bolton team that included seven Scots and two Welshmen.

Darwen's Lancashire Cup Final Team of 1890/91
Top: JW Smith, Haddow, Leach, W Marsden, J Marsden
Bottom: R Smith, Thornber, Entwistle, Owen, McOwen, Nightingale
(source: Yore Publications)

Comtemporary notes on the 1890/91 team *(source Yore Publications):*

John Ralph Leach: Full back. A man of few words and assuming manner - respected by all. A good tackler with rare judgement.

William McOwen: Goalkeeper. 20 yrs old possesses a high amount of pluck. Has a strong kick and can clear his goal in any position.

Joseph Marsden: 22yrs old Captain. Not weighty but plays a fine game, kicks powerfully for one so light, does not leave an opponent until either beaten or has got the ball

Jim Haddow: Left half back, 19 yrs old. A reserve player brought in to cover T Marsden's injury.

David Owen: 26 yr old centre-half. A thorn in the side of many a centre forward.

Richard Thornber: right half back. Is of "rollicking disposition", and a "tough 'un" to deal with. General favourite with the crowd.

W Marsden: Centre forward, 19 yrs old. Possesses rare pluck and any quantity of "go". Ever ready to tackle the biggest antagonist. Holds his wings together well and is well qualified for his position.

Jonathan Entwistle: Outside left, 25 years old, very speedy and runs strongly, when once clear he is bad to get at and he goes for goal with a vengeance as the "North End" know...

R Smith: Inside right 21 yrs old. Has amply justified his place in replacing Fish in the Darwen forward line

JW Smith: Inside left- not a brilliant or individual man on the field but is a tryer and plods along from beginning to end

Jimmy Nightingale: Outside right, oldest in the team at 27. All but indispensable forward. Has of a turn of speed which is almost unequalled, while his centring is well timed and pretty accurate.

***

In 1892 Darwen once again reached the semi final of the cup and were, again, drawn against Blackburn Rovers. The game at Ewood Park ended in a 1-1 draw but Darwen were unable to capitalise on home advantage for the replay, losing 3-2 at Barley Bank.

1891: Another Cap

Despite Darwen's relatively uninspiring form in the Football Alliance, several of their players were still regular choices for the Lancashire county side at that time.

The club's outstanding Lancashire Cup run of 1890/91 brought to prominence Darwen's team captain of the time, Marsden, to such an extent that he was awarded an England cap.

Joseph Thomas Marsden was born in Darwen in 1868. He played for the Royal Blues, Hibernians and Padiham before signing for Darwen.

Joseph Marsden wearing a Lancashire County Cap
(source: Blackburn with Darwen Library & Information Service)

His big day came on 7th March 1891 when England played Ireland in a Home International Championship game at Wolverhampton. England won the match 6-1 and, by all accounts, Marsden played rather well. Many observers were, therefore, disappointed that he did not appear in England's next match - against Scotland at Ewood Park - although he was named as a reserve.

Following his elevation to stardom, Marsden soon joined Everton. He played for them in the first League match of the 1891/92 against West Bromwich Albion and then mysteriously quit the game.

Douglas Lamming describes the right back as " *on the light size, but wonderfully clever and possesses great judgement. The last, by a decade,- of Darwen's four England caps. And, on a sad note, was yet another of the early internationals to die at a young age*". He died in 1897, aged 29.

Season 1891/92 - Football League At Last

For the 1891/92 season, it was decided to expand the Football League by an additional two teams - from its original 12 to 14.

The League's bottom four clubs from the 1890/91 season had to apply for re-election and 6 hopeful candidates joined them in the draw for the 6 places that would be available in the newly expanded league. The four existing Football League clubs - West Bromwich Albion, Aston Villa, Accrington and Derby County - were all re-elected to the league and were joined by Darwen and Stoke.

Stoke had actually been one of the founder members of the league but had been voted off in favour of Sunderland after finishing bottom two seasons running. They had played the previous season in the Football Alliance instead, finishing in top spot.

Despite having only finished in 6th place in the Football Alliance for the second season running, Darwen actually pooled the third highest vote tally of all 10 candidates in the draw. Sunderland Albion - who many had expected to be elected - missed out, as did Nottingham Forest and Newton Heath.

Although hard to understand from a distance of some 120 years, the reason for this may in fact, be quite an obvious one. With so many other Lancashire clubs already playing in the League, the attraction of having two more derby matches per season - with their guaranteed high attendances - would be justification enough to vote for Darwen instead of a more distantly situated team such as Sunderland or Nottingham.

For their debut season in the Football League, Darwen were told that they would have to change their playing colours as their black and white stripes clashed with those of Notts. County.The search for new playing colours came up with an unusual combination - salmon and blue. However, Howard Peters suggests that salmon was not such an unlikely choice as "salmons" was already in common usage as a nickname for Darwen people at that time.

Apparently this originally came from a type of cheap dog fish that people used to eat and which often scornfully referred to as a "Darwen salmon". Thus the Darwen club acquired a nickname - *The Salmoners* - which is still sometimes used to this day.

Darwen's first ever game in the Football League took place on 5th September 1891 at Barley Bank where they entertained Bolton Wanderers. A huge 7,000 crowd turned out to watch the "Salmoners" in their new salmon shirts and indigo shorts lose 1-2.

The Darwen team for that historic match was: McOwen, Leach, Simmons, Thornber, Owen, Haddow, Alexander, Heap, Smith, Carty, Entwhistle. The Darwen goal was scored by Jonty Entwistle.

2 days later, on 7th September, the team travelled to Everton and lost 3-5 and a further defeat followed away at Bolton before Darwen finally managed to notch up their first win - 5-2 at home to Accrington on 19th September.

That victory lifted Darwen off the bottom of the league table and a 2-2 draw at Wolverhampton and a high scoring 9-3 thrashing of fellow strugglers Stoke elevated them briefly to the dizzy heights of 5th place.

However, that run of success was very short-lived and the draw at Wolves and a 1-1 draw away at Accrington in mid October were the only away points of the whole season.

A run of 3 straight defeats was ended on November 14th with a surprise 3 -1 home win over reigning champions Everton but, from then on, the best League position that Darwen could manage for the rest of the campaign was 11th.

The Salmoners' last League win of the season came at home to Derby County on 28th November and, after that, they only picked up one solitary point from their remaining 13 games - a 1-1 draw at home to West Bromwich Albion who, strangely enough, had beaten them 12-0 away a fortnight earlier.

Other heavy defeats included 7-0 scorelines away at Derby, Sunderland and Aston Villa and 9-0 at Burnley. Not surprisingly, the team finished bottom of the Football League with a record of Played 26 Won 4 Drawn 3 Lost 19 and a goal difference of 38:112

This time around there were no extended cup runs to keep the fans cheerful and the Darreners were knocked out of the FA Cup by Aston Villa in the second round. They also missed out on a place in the final of the Lancashire Cup losing the semi final 3-2 at home to Blackburn Rovers.

The club chairman blamed his players bad performances on the effects of excessive alcohol and that they were *"not training sufficiently but spending their time in pubs from morning till night."* He subsequently asked for club members to stop treating players to drinks.

At the end of the season the four bottom clubs in the League - Accrington (20pts), West Bromwich (18pts), Stoke (14pts) and Darwen (11pts) - all had to apply for re-election.

Although the other three clubs were voted back in, Darwen were rejected, despite the fact that the League was going to be extended to 16 clubs for the following season. Nottingham Forest and Newton Heath, who finished first and second in the Football Alliance, were voted in to the League along with Sheffield Wednesday.

However, in addition to extending the Football League to 16 teams, it had also been decided to form a second division from the rest of Football Alliance teams and, thus, Darwen were able to become founder members of the new Football League Division Two.

Season 1892/93 - Division Two

Darwen began preparations for the 1892/93 season with a warm up game against Blackburn Rovers and notched up an unexpected 2-1 win.

In the first Division Two game of the season, the Darwen side - now playing in plain white shirts - travelled away to Walsall Town Swifts, where they picked up a morale boosting 2-1 win. However, in the second game of the campaign, they lost at home to Burton Swifts 3-2 but that was to be the only home defeat all season in the league and, indeed, the only points dropped at Barley Bank.

Four home wins on the trot followed and, by the end of October, Darwen were sitting proudly on top of the Division Two table.

On 10th December they entertained Small Heath in a top of the table clash at Barley Bank. The Birmingham team, who went on to be champions that season, scored a goal direct from the kick off. Darwen protested in vain that it had been offside and then had two goals of their own disallowed before the break. After a valiant second half fight-back, the Darreners eventually won the game 4-3

An FA Cup Interlude

In January 1893, the FA Cup provided more excitement for the Barley Bank fans as Darwen were drawn against Aston Villa in the first round for the second year running.

The Villa team that day included some great players of the day such as Athersmith, Devey, and Dennis Hodgetts

Speaking some 50 years after the event, Alderman Taylor - a stalwart of the Darwen club for many years - remembered this as the first game he saw at Barley Bank : *"I didn't get on the ground until half time when they used to let we lads in for a penny. Villa were then winning 3-1. Five minutes from the end they were still on top although Darwen had fought back a bit to make it 4-3.*

Jonty Entwistle
(source:Blackburn with Darwen
Library & Information Service)

"Then somebody gave two wonderful passes to Jonty Entwistle on the wing. Now Jonty was not a ball player but he was a grand runner. He could give yards away to the full back marking him. He put over two great centres and McKennie the centre forward netted the ball from both to win the match in the nick of time."

An alternative retrospective account of the match in the *Darwen News* has Entwistle scoring the winning goal himself being *"pursued by a fox terrier whilst making for the goal"* which does, in fact, create a more entertaining image.

Darwen's team that day was: Kenyon (goal); Leach & Orr (backs); Fish, Maxwell and McAvoy (half backs); Wade, WC Campbell, McKenna, Sutherland, Entwistle (forwards).

They beat Grimsby 2-0 in the second round before losing out to eventual winners Wolverhampton Wanderers 5-0 in the next round. However that game also had a memorable end to it, as Alderman Taylor continues:

"Wade...was a neat little player who never used to think of fouling his opponent whereas Campbell was a big tough fellow. If Wade got bumped by an opponent, Campbell would be on his track.

JJ Wade
(source:
Blackburn with
Darwen Library
& Information
Service)

WC Campbell
(source:Blackburn with Darwen Library & Information Service)

The Wanderers' famous centre half Malpass knocked Wade off the ball and the Darwen player split his knee open on the icy ground. Campbell did not bother about this incident until the game was nearly over and he made his way deliberately towards Malpass with the ball.

Then, just as the final whistle blowing he gave Malpass "a clout like Rocky Marciano" and knocked him out cold."

(Note: Alderman Taylor actually stated that this incident occurred during a 2-2 draw but the only draw on record between Darwen and Wolverhampton Wanderers was in a Football League match on 28th September 1891 - but Campbell was not playing for Darwen at the time. The only time when all three players appear to have been on the pitch at the same time would have been this 5-0 FA Cup defeat in February 1893)

Wade later signed for Blackburn Rovers but had to retire early after another knee injury.

JR Leach
(source: Blackburn with Darwen Library & Information Service)

Speaking of other players from that era, Alderman Taylor remembers Sutherland as *"one of the bonniest ball players there were"* and further comments that *"John Ralph Leach was the greatest right back that never played for England. His sense of timing when a winger was coming up with the ball was uncanny"*

I cannot ever remember him charging a player. He used to turn and slide the ball right from their toes. He was, in my opinion, a greater full back than Bob Crompton of Blackburn Rovers."

Just prior to joining Darwen from Kilmarnock, James Orr played for Scotland starring in a 6-1 British International Championship win over Wales in March 1892.

The Promotion Test Match

Darwen Football Club 1892-93
Back: Grime, Leach, Kenyon, Orr / Middle: Entwistle, Fish, Maxell,
McAvoy / Front: Wade, Campbell, McKennie, Sutherland, Lofthouse
(source: Blackburn with Darwen Library Information Service)

Although practically unbeatable at home in the League, the team's away form was less consistent and a disappointing record of 4 wins from their 11 away games meant that Darwen were only able to finish third in the final Division 2 table. However, they did top the crowd figures for second division attendances with the highest overall average of 3,500 for the season.

That final league placing - 5 points behind runners up Sheffield United and 7 ahead of 4th place Grimsby Town - meant that Darwen qualified for the promotion/relegation test matches that had been introduced for that season to decide which teams would be play in Division One the following year (there was no such thing as automatic promotion and relegation at that time).

The play off match took place on 22nd April 1892 on a neutral ground - Ardwick's Hyde Road home in Manchester - and Darwen were faced with the difficult task of playing Notts County who had finished 3rd from bottom in Division One and were, consequently, thought of as the team most likely to stay up of the three relegation candidates.

The Darwen line-up for the big game was more or less the same as had played consistently well together for most of the season, with the successful striking partnership of McKennie (15 goals) and Sutherland (12) leading the attack.

But, by half time the main prong of the Darwen attack had failed to break through and they were trailing by two goals to one, Maxwell being the Darwen goalscorer. After the break, centre half David Owen, who had only played twice during the league campaign, pulled a goal back.

Then another player, whose name history has failed to record, scored a third goal for Darwen. The defence held strong and kept the Notts County forwards at bay.

The final score of 3-1 meant that Darwen had won promotion to the First Division at the first time of asking and brought to a close what would turn out to be - although no-one could have known it at the time - the club's best ever, and only really successful, season in the Football League.

Ironically, Division Two champions Small Heath lost their test match with First Division Newton Heath and, as such, the champions failed to win promotion.

Season 1893/94 - Back in the Top Flight

Darwen Football Club 1893-94
Back: Geo. Briggs, Leach, Kenyon, Maxwell, Fish, Hunter
Middle: Wade, McKenny, McKnight, McAvoy, Simpson
Front: Orr, Sutherland
(source: Darwen Football Club)

Darwen prepared for the new season back in the First Division by taking on several new players to strengthen the team that had just won promotion. The most notable of these was a forward called McKnight who would go on to be the club's top goal scorer for 1893/94.

The first league game of the new campaign on 2nd September brought local rivals Blackburn Rovers to Barley Bank. Unfortunately, the new boys weren't able to get off to a winning start as they narrowly lost 2-3.

New signing McKnight then got into his stride and scored in each of the next three games but the Darwen fans had to wait until the 4th game of the season before they could see a win. That finally came at the expense of Stoke City as Darwen triumphed 3-1.

On 18th September, they lost 2-1 away at Wolverhampton. As was often the case in those days, and, indeed, is just as true today, the club blamed the referee for the defeat. Following the game they took the step of reporting the referee, a Mr Jeffreys, for *"general incompetence"* and having been *"under the influence of alcohol"*.

Not surprisingly, this did not go down at all well with the Football League management committee. Darwen later withdrew the alcohol claim and, following further discussions where little evidence could be found of the other charge, the matter was dropped altogether, and Darwen had to publicly apologise to Mr Jeffreys.

In the first half of the season, Darwen won just 3 and drew 1 of their 15 games. Although many of the defeats were close, Darwen were bottom of the table by November and it was, again, apparent that they couldn't really keep up with the big teams anymore.

In the run up to Christmas they beat Sheffield Wednesday at home 2-1 and then drew 1-1 away at West Bromwich Albion but the three fixtures over the Christmas period all saw defeats - including a 9-0 hammering away at eventual champions Aston Villa on Boxing Day.

From their last 10 games of the season, Darwen did manage two more wins - over Preston North End and Wolverhampton - but they lost all of their last 4 games and finished second from bottom, 5 points ahead of basement club Newton Heath.

For the second season running, Darwen found themselves involved in the test match, this time for the wrong reasons. The game was played at Stoke's Victoria Ground on 28th April against Second Division runners up Small Heath. McKnight scored in the first half for Darwen but the Birmingham side were too strong and won the game 3-1 to send Darwen back down to Division 2.

Season 1894/95

The talk of the town in July 1984 was the arrival at Darwen Football Club of former England international forward William Townley (right).

William Townley
(source: Darwen FC)

He had played as a centre forward with Blackburn Olympic and Blackburn Rovers and scored a hat-trick in the 1890 FA Cup final.

Townley was brought in to replace McKnight who, presumably, didn't fancy the idea of Second Division football.

The season started off in bright fashion with a 5-0 win over Newcastle United at Barley Bank on 1st September. A week later Darwen beat Lincoln city 6-0 at home to lead the Second Division table.

On their travels they picked up away wins at Manchester City (4-2) and Burslem Port Vale (3-0) and did not lose a game at home until the visit of eventual champions Bury on 15th December.

After that, they did not lose another home game all season but just one single away win in the second half of the campaign - 2-0 at Lincoln - meant that Darwen slowly began to slip down the table. At the end of March they were 4th but by the end of the season they had slipped down to 6th place, albeit just 2 points away from a test match spot. Townley ended up top scorer, level with Maxwell on 12 goals each.

Not for the first time, nor the last, a meeting was held at the end of April to discuss the club's finances. Despite a reasonable season they had made a loss of £240 as the gate money received hadn't covered the wage bill and it was decided to disband the reserve side in an attempt to cut costs.

Season 1895/96

In 1895 Darwen signed Jimmy Forrest from Blackburn Rovers. He had been the first professional player to appear for England against Scotland in 1886 and made 8 appearances overall in an England jersey.

Jimmy Forrest
(source: Darwen FC)

Forrest fell out with the Rovers towards the end of his career and decided to join Darwen. His arrival was such a coup that he was carried around the town on the shoulders of the excited Darwen fans.

The League campaign started with a 0-3 defeat away at Burton Wanderers but, overall, the season went well for Darwen. Once again, they lost just one home game all season - 0-4 to Liverpool who, like Bury the previous year, would go on to be champions. They notched up some impressive victories at home, including 8-2 over Port Vale, 6-1 over Crewe and 10-2 over Rotherham, and an early season League double over Leicester suggested that things were on the up.

Then in February, it was announced that the club was in serious financial difficulties and was in danger of folding there and then. The question of forming a limited company and selling shares to raise capital was mooted but not followed up. Somehow or other, the club managed to struggle on to the end of the season.

On the pitch, the team lost 4 of their last 10 games, picking up two away wins to finish off the season but, despite this late rally, the best they could manage in the league table was a 9th place finish.

Jimmy Forrest made just 10 appearances for the club, scoring 1 goal before retiring. Charles Townley played for most of the season but had obviously lost his touch in front of goal, scoring just 3 times in 17 games. He moved to Manchester City and later coached abroad.

Season 1896/97

In order to try and attract the crowds back to Barley Bank, much work was done during the summer months in preparation for the new season. The ground was repainted, new fences erected and extra crowd accommodation added behind the goals. Turnstiles were added at the entrances to the ground to save time issuing tickets.

The club had imported a group of Scottish players to strengthen the team and large crowd was present at Darwen station to greet two of them - Murray and Reid - even though they arrived very late at night. Another player - Nixon, a Yorkshireman - chose to join Darwen over Woolwich Arsenal such was the pulling power of the club even at that time.

In a preseason friendly, a win 4-1 over Rock Ferry suggested that good times were ahead but unfortunately, Darwen then lost their first League match of the season 4-1 away to Leicester Fosse. The new Scottish players did not seem to be up to scratch after all and, in September, were ordered to *"get into a better physical condition and to pay more attention to training"*.

Two of the Scots - Reid and Porteous - got into more trouble straight away for missing the train to an away game and, in mid September, they and two more of their countrymen packed their bags and went back to Scotland. As they waited on Darwen station they held an impromptu press conference where they cited the committee's criticism and being forced to play out of position as their reasons for leaving.

In the wake of the Scots' departure, the committee accepted that the idea to use them had been a mistake and that they had *"neither the ability nor the inclination to serve the club nobly"*.

Unfortunately, this lack of discipline seems to have been a common problem at the time, and not just restricted to the Scottish players. In August 1896, Hunt was censured for selfish play and in October he was in trouble again and told that *"he must not change his position without the consent of the captain"*.

Hunt was one of the team top wage earners at the time, earning, along with John Ralph Leach, £2 10s a week. He was described as *"a temperamental player - brilliant one day and abysmal the next""* and in December he was told by the directors that *"the less he had to do with bookmakers the better"*.

Team performances plummeted further and players were signed and released with increasing regularity. As club morale worsened, many players were suspended for misconduct. Nixon and Lees were both suspended for a month.

The club was still in dire financial straits and finding it ever harder to compete with the bigger teams in the league. Aston Villa, for example, had moved to a new stadium and were regularly attracting crowds of 70,000, compared to Darwen's 2,000 or so.

The committee were always looking for ways to cut costs and one of them came in the shape of travelling on the day of the game in order to avoid paying out for hotel bills.

In September they travelled to Newcastle United for an away match and the players had to leave Darwen on the 5.48am train. The score was level at half time at 1-1 but Darwen eventually lost the game 5-1, collapsing in the second half. The press put this down to tiredness from the journey and, as the Darreners beat Newcastle at home in the return game, this could well have been the case.

A similar thing happened a few days later when they travelled to Luton - again on the day of the game - and finished up 5-0 losers after having only been one goal down at half time.

In November, the player Crook needed a new pair of football boots but the club was so badly off that they couldn't pay for them. The player was sent down to the shop with a promissary note stating that the boots would be paid for out of the takings at the forthcoming Saturday's game.

By Christmas the directors realised that the only way to generate some cash would be to sell some players to cut the wage bill and, a few days later, Nixon - arguably the club's best player at the time - was sold to Bolton Wanderers for £30.

Despite all the unfortunate goings on off the pitch, Darwen still managed to win some games and lost only two games at home all season - 2-3 to Blackpool and 0-2 to Newton Heath. On Boxing Day 1896, they recorded their best ever win in the Football League - 12-0 over Walsall Town Swifts, although the visitors did only field 8 men for the whole match.

The New Year brought home wins over teams that would become huge names in later years - 4-1 over Woolwich Arsenal on 1st January 1897 and 3-1 over Manchester City on 9th January but, overall, it was the away form that prevented Darwen from making a success of the season.

They won just once away from home - a 4-2 win over Gainsborough on Christmas Day and, other than that, did not pick up a single point on their travels. Unfortunately, Darwen had three away games in a row to finish the season off and lost all three without scoring a single goal. In the end they finished up in a safe but disappointing 11th place in the Second Division.

An interesting fact is that they did not register a single draw all season and, to this day, Darwen's 1896/97 season remains the only time that this has occurred in the Football League.

Darwen's
Draw
Record
(source: Bob Eccles)

Season 1897/98

In the run up to the new season, Darwen Football Club had finally become a limited company in order to try and stabilise the club's finances. Unfortunately, the 1897/98 season turned out to be the worst yet and the club finished second bottom of the Second Division, winning just 6 and drawing 1 of their 30 games.

Four of those wins came at home in the early part of the season: 3-2 v Lincoln, 2-1 v Loughborough, 1-0 v Grimsby and 3-1 v Blackpool when optimism was still high but 5 defeats on the trot in December and January put paid to any chances of promotion.

There followed two surprise away wins - at bottom placed Loughborough and at Leicester Fosse - but a terrible record of 11 straight defeats in their last 11 games saw Darwen having to apply for re-election. In the event they just managed to avoid finishing bottom because of a superior goal difference over Loughborough of -45 as opposed to -63.

The Football League meeting took place on 20th May in Manchester. Along with Darwen, Lincoln City and Loughborough were also seeking re-election and there was added competition from new applicants Burslem Port Vale, Bristol City, Nelson and New Brighton, who also went into the ballot for the three available positions.

When the votes were counted, the shock news was that Darwen had been outvoted by Port Vale and would lose their place in the Second Division. However, the very next item on the agenda at the meeting was a move to extend both divisions by two teams from 16 to 18. This motion was carried and Darwen were granted a reprieve and offered a place in the extended Second Division for the following season.

Season 1898/99

Before the season had even started, Darwen Football Club found itself at a disadvantage when it was discovered that many home games would clash with Blackburn Rovers' First Division fixtures at Ewood Park. As Darwen were already struggling to attract decent crowds, competition like that would probably have meant the end of the road for the club there and then.

Luckily, Blackburn agreed to change some of their dates and the problem was lessened. On 14th June 1898 it was recorded that Blackpool would be offered a player on a free transfer - Spinks - if they also agreed to a change of fixtures.

But no amount of juggling with the fixture list could make up for the fact that Darwen were, by now, a struggling team. They started the season with three straight defeats and, by Christmas, the team was bottom of the table with just 4 points, and just one win - at home to Leicester Fosse. They had scored just 12 goals and conceded 75

During that season Darwen used an amazing 63 different players for their league matches. Defeat followed defeat on the pitch and, off it, club discipline continued to be a huge problem.

Many players would turn up for training and receive their money but suddenly produce a sick wife or relative on the occasion of an away game. The club records carry an instruction from that time that one player - Wain - was not to be selected for away games, presumably because he never showed up. This was an important issue as the club tended not to take extra players to an away game and if one of the 11 did not show they had to play with just 10 men.

On one such occasion in November, even the *Darwen News* reporter RE Yates was called upon to make up the numbers for the game away at Small Heath when no last minute replacement could be found. Darwen lost 8-0 although there is no reason to suggest that this was purely down to the presence of the journalist in the team.

High scoring thrashings became the norm as the season wore on. Darwen conceded 20 goals in three games in the run up to Christmas, including a 0-9 drubbing away at Newton Heath, during a period where they went 7 games without scoring a goal. In the second half of the season, things got even worse and they lost 10-0 away from home on three separate occasions - at Woolwich Arsenal, Manchester City and Loughborough Town.

While all those problems were continuing on the field of play, the field itself had also become a bit of a worry.

The Lord of the Manor - Reverend Duckworth - wanted to sell off some of the Barley Bank field to enable an extension to Hindle Street and an addition to Barley Bank Street on the east side. This would have meant removing the cricket pavilion and the football grandstand, the latter being roughly in line with Hindle Street.

After much debate and various counter proposals, he eventually agreed to allow the club to stay as it was for two more seasons.

Building Proposals for Barley Bank
(source: Blackburn with Darwen Library & Information Service)

A further hammer blow came when a player called Grier, who had since moved to Preston North End, decided to sue Darwen Football Club for his back wages. The club did not have any funds to pay him so he sent in the bailiffs.

After attempts at mediation, all of which failed, an auction was held at Barley Bank to sell off the club's fixtures and fittings in order to make a settlement.

All the players' equipment went, as did the dressing tents and even the metal railings around the pitch went under the auctioneers hammer but, by the time all the legal costs had been met, there was very little money left over for Grier.

Surrounded by desolation, Darwen played Luton Town on 1st April and notched up a surprising 4-1 win - their first victory since Leicester's visit on 1st October. The upsurge did not last long however and Darwen returned to their more regular form 4 days later with a 2-9 defeat away at Grimsby.

With just two wins and three draws to their credit all season, there was no doubt that Darwen would finish anywhere other than bottom of the league table. They finished up with the unenviable record of the highest number of goals ever conceded in the Football League - 141 in 34 games. This "feat" has never been equalled.

With no money, practically no ground and no likelihood of being re-elected, it was clear to all that the club had come to the end of the road. A special shareholders meeting was held on 20th April where it was agreed that *"the old club be allowed to die and a new club be formed and seek admission to the Lancashire League"*.

Darwen Football Club's last ever game in the Football League took place on 22nd April 1899 when they entertained Newton Heath at Barley Bank.

The Darwen team that day was: McIvor (goal), Woolfall and Cawthorne (backs), Moore, Livesey and Ratcliffe (half backs), Wilson, Bleasdale, Pilkington, Eccles and Collinson (forwards).

1,000 spectators turned out to watch the Darrerners' swansong and, judging on past results, would have been rather surprised when Darwen took a first half lead through Pilkington somewhat against the run of play.

In the second half Newton Heath hit back and equalised but the newspaper reports suggest that the Darwen players did not lose heart and might have scored a well deserved winner before the end. In the event, neither team could break the deadlock. The final score was 1-1 and Darwen went out of the Football League on a relative high note.

Following the club's decision to drop out of the Football League and to reform, the landlord decided not to renew their lease at Barley Bank after all. As they were unable to pay the asking price to buy the freehold, they had to look for a new home. Two possible sites were looked at - Ellison Field and Heyfold - but the committee eventually plumped for the Anchor.

The grandstand still remained in place at Barley Bank and there were plans to move it to the new ground. However, the structure belonged to a private company of sponsors who had helped pay for it to be built, and that represented yet another financial headache for the ailing club.

The committee's earlier decision was ratified at a further meeting on 15th May 1899, where it was formally agreed that the club should go into liquidation after a friendly game against Burnley.

FROM THE INDEPENDENT 23/8/2003

Darwen's theory of losing under threat

▶ SO SUNDERLAND are one defeat away from equalling the longest losing run in English League history. Their defeat to Millwall last week was their 17th straight loss. Now only Darwen's mark of 18, set in 1898-99, has to be beaten to guarantee infamy. Mick McCarthy's side face Preston today and Watford on Monday. Yet things could be worse. When Darwen set the record they were suffering from dwindling support, loss of personnel and indiscipline. They used 63 players in that campaign 105

years ago, including a local journalist. They conceded 141 league goals (109 away from home, including three 10-0 drubbings), a record that still stands.

Sunderland can take solace in having Darwen's support in their mission to avoid the record. Darwen's chairwoman, Kath Marah, said the record is part of her club's rich history and she wants to keep it. Not that she will be paying too much attention to Sunderland today. Darwen are starting their FA Cup campaign in the extra preliminary round at Fleetwood Town.

Chapter Three: Into Lancashire

No sooner had the old Darwen Football Club been wound up, than plans were already being set in motion to set up its successor. A public meeting on 3rd May in the Industrial Hall agreed to form a new organisation, again using the name "Darwen Football Club".

A new management committee was elected and initial resolutions were passed that the club's expenses were to be kept down to £15.00 per week and no summer wages would be paid to players.

Councillor Walter Knowles JP was the only member of the old club board to be elected to the new club and remained a director until the First World War. He later became mayor of Darwen.

In the weeks that followed further meetings appointed Mr AW Huntington as President of the new club and Thomas Hindle as Treasurer.

There was a lot of discussion as to which league the new club should join but most were in favour of the professional Lancashire League. It makes very interesting reading to see what the *Darwen News* of the time had to say on the subject:

"The more Lancashire clubs there are that find themselves at the bottom of the First League (Football League), the sooner will the Lancashire League be looked to as the more suitable combination to join. With the Southern League at one end and the Lancashire League at the other, there seems every possibility that the Second Division will eventually go to the wall."

Of course, in some ways, this prediction did come true but, instead of the lower section of the Football League collapsing, it actually grew stronger with the incorporation of the Southern League as a Third Division in 1920.

Background to the various leagues

The Lancashire League was formed in 1888/89 to offer a league structure for the other teams in Lancashire that did not qualify for either the Football League or the Football Alliance.

These initially included eventual league teams such as Blackpool, Bury, and Liverpool but the highly prestigious Lancashire League absolutely refused to accept membership application from reserve sides of league clubs. Because of this, a group of league sides including Blackburn Rovers, Bolton Wanderers and Preston North End set up their own rival competition - the Lancashire Combination - for the 1891/92 season.

However, the situation soon reversed itself as the leading Lancashire League clubs gradually began to win election to the Football League and the competition began to lose its attraction, suffering declining attendances.

Ironically the clubs that had earlier wanted to exclude the reserve sides of Football League clubs then suddenly decided that it would be better to be playing in the same league as them after all and most of them then decided to switch over the to the Lancashire Combination. The Lancashire League continued to decline as more and more of its members joined the Combination and, in the end, the clubs that remained were transferred in en bloc and a second division was added to the Combination in 1903/04 to cope with the extra number of clubs.

However, the newly found status quo did not last long. In May 1911, once again outnumbered by the non-league clubs, the Football League reserve sides found that they kept getting outvoted on various issues and, once again, began to feel aggrieved. As a result they broke away to form the Central League.

A few seasons later, the Cheshire clubs left the Combination en masse to form the Cheshire County League and the Combination suffered further when many of the top clubs were drafted into the 3rd Division North of the Football League in 1921.

A New Start For Darwen FC

The field that was to become the Anchor Ground was attached to the Anchor Farm and had previously been open pasture.

The new club initially leased it at a rent of £10 from 1st September to 30th April inclusive, with a separate agreement regarding practice matches in August.

At the beginning of August 1899, arrangements were made to transfer the grandstand from Barley Bank over to the Anchor Ground. The tenant of the farm - Mr Dick Smith - who was subletting the field to the club, kindly loaned them the sum of £100.00 to buy to the stand shareholders and pay for the move.

The new club colours were also decided upon. These were to be *"turkey red and black striped"* shirts with blue shorts.

The club started its new life in the Lancashire League in thrifty style. For an away trip to Stockport County, the players had to walk from Manchester Victoria station to Manchester Piccadilly (or London Road as it was then known) and then again from Heaton Norris station to the Stockport ground. Not surprisingly, they lost the match 3-0.

By Christmas the Darreners were third in the table and getting reasonable gates at their new home, even though it was much more difficult to get to than Barley Bank had been.

They were drawn against local rivals Chorley in both the Lancashire and FA Cups and took each to a replay before succumbing in both. Overall, life was not quite as easy in the lower league as many might have expected. Gone were the big name players and the ex internationals. Gone were the expensive imports. The club was now based firmly on more locally based talent but, come the end of the season, Darwen could only manage 5th place out of 15 teams, having won 13 of their 28 games.

The 1900/01 season was much the same although they improved slightly on their league position, finishing 4th, albeit in a weakened league of only 11 teams, winning 10 of 20 matches.

There was, however, one piece of silverware to celebrate as Darwen FC beat the mighty Blackburn Rovers at Ewood Park to win the East Lancashire Charity Shield. The origins of this trophy are not clear nor are the details of the match, other than the fact that the Rovers team that day boasted many prestigious international players, including the legendary Bob Crompton.

Season 1901-02

After two mid-table seasons, during which time the Anchor Ground was being made to look more like a football arena than a cowfield, the 1901/02 season was the one when everything finally fell into place.

Darwen got the new season off to the best start possible when on 29th October 1901 they overcame Football League rivals Burnley 2-1 after two replays to win the prestigious East Lancs Charity Cup.

They built on this to make an unbeaten start to the league campaign and, at the same time, saw off Blackpool, Southport and Nelson to reach the 1st round proper of the FA Cup. They were drawn at home to Woolwich Arsenal and some 7,000 fans - Darwen's biggest crowd for years - packed into the Anchor Ground to watch the spectacle.

The Darwen team for the match was: McIvor (goal); Collinson and Haslam (backs); Bridge, Walker, R Kenyon (half backs); Humphreys, Cooper, Hulligan, B Gates and Leeming (forwards).

In the event the minnows lost the game 2-0 but were unlucky to do so. Beaten in the FA Cup but still unbeaten in the league, Darwen managed to go the whole season without a defeat.

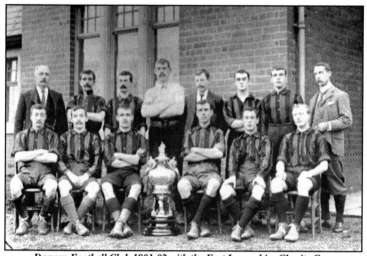

Darwen Football Club 1901-02 with the East Lancashire Charity Cup
Back: W Todd, Bridge, Halsam, Arnott, Knowles, Pomfret, Pollard, Eccles
Front: Duckworth, Cooper, Walker, Hulligan, Quinn, Dawson
(source: Marjorie Bibby)

They ended up champions of the Lancashire League with a record of P24 W 18 D6 L0, finishing 6 points ahead of Southport Central.

One of their key players was inside right Daniel Cooper who was one of the leading goalscorers that season.

Writing some 50 years later, Alderman Taylor, a lifelong stalwart of the Darwen club, said of him: "*Danny was one of the best little players I have ever known. He would have been a celebrity in football had he not had such bad luck with his health and had to retire so early. He was not big but he had one of the strongest shots I have ever seen on a football ground.*"

Recalling the FA Cup tie with Woolwich Arsenal on 5th January 1901, he said: "*Darwen completely outplayed the London side. They lost to two of the softest goals I have ever seen!*"

60

Cooper went on to play for Accrington Stanley and Stalybridge and carried on working locally until he was well into his 70s. His granddaughter, Marjorie Bibby, remembers that he always spoke with great pride about his footballing days but that he also put great emphasis on his family life. He married Elizabeth Kay in 1902 and after the birth of their daughter Edith, his playing commitments took second place.

Daniel Cooper died in the early 1960s and his winner's medals were callously stolen from Mrs Bibby's home in 1993.

Above: Daniel Cooper at Barley Bank
Right Representation of Daniel Cooper's
Lancashire League winners medal based
on a description by Marjorie Bibby

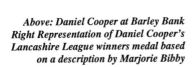

The following season Darwen were once again triumphant in the East Lancs Charity Cup, beating Accrington Stanley 2-1 in a closely fought final on 6th December 1902. They were not, however, able to replicate their league success of the previous season and finished runners up in the Lancashire League, 5 points behind champions Southport Central. That was their last year in the Lancashire League and, in common with many of the other leading clubs, they switched over to the Lancashire Combination for the following season.

The Lancashire Combination

A Darwen team had played in the Lancashire Combination in seasons 1892/93 and 1893/4 finishing 2nd and 3rd in the table respectively. It may well have been that the club used these extra fixtures to pad out their competitive fixtures and this argument is borne out by the fact that, in the following season, the Palatine League was created by the other League clubs for this same purpose.

Certainly in the 1894/95 season the Darwen team was now called Darwen Reserves and this team played in the Combination until finances became too stretched for it to continue.

The senior Darwen side joined the Combination for the 1903/04 season and they met with reasonable success. They finished 5th of 18 teams twice in a row in 1903/04 and 1904/05 and the following season were runners up to Accrington Stanley.

Then the club's fortunes went into freefall as, in successive seasons, they finished 7th 16th and then 17th in Combination. That final performance was enough to see them relegated to the Second Division at the end of the 1908/09 season.

If anyone had been hoping for a quick return to the top flight, they would have been very disappointed with the first season down in Division 2. A terrible run saw Darwen win only 13 of their 34 games against, supposedly, lower quality opposition and they ended up in 17th place out of 20 teams.

Luckily, that was the lowest the club dropped in footballing terms but, despite still attracting crowds of around 2,000, financial problems were never far away. Not for the first time, the reserve team was disbanded to save costs and it was only due to the timely - albeit catastrophic - intervention of World War 1 that saved Darwen Football Club from drifting further into obscurity.

The Combination carried on in various formats throughout the war years but Darwen did not play again until 1920.

Notable Players Of The Pre-WW1 Period

Now playing in a lower league, Darwen had to make do with using young up and coming local talent or the occasional big name star who was at the end of his career. Here are a few such players:

Edgar Chadwick. Born Blackburn 1869. had an outstanding Football League career with Everton, Burnley, Liverpool & Blackpool. Played 7 times for England during 1891-97 while at Everton. Joined Darwen in 1906. Later coached in Germany and Holland.

Albert Walmsley. Born Blackburn 1885. Played for Darwen in 1905/06 and 1906/07 before moving to Blackburn Rovers where he won two championships in 1911 and 1913.

Horace Fairhurst. Born Bolton 1895. Played for Darwen in the pre war period. Signed professionally for Blackpool in 1919. Died aged 26 after a bad knock on the head in a game against Barnsley on Boxing Day 1920.

Samuel Wadsworth. Born Darwen 1896. Left back. Played for Darwen before the Great War. Went on to be an FA Cup winner with Huddersfield in the 1920s, making 9 appearances for England.

The 1920s - A Renaissance Period

Partially as a result of the departure of the league clubs' reserve teams in the years before the war and also due to the inability of some clubs to get reorganised after it, the Lancashire Combination reverted to a single division competition, which Darwen rejoined for the 1920/21 season.

Before them lay a programme of rebuilding, not just of the team but also the ground, as the *Northern Daily Telegraph* observed: " *the ground at the Anchor was barren land, everything that had furnished it before the war having disappeared*".

In all, the 1920s were good for Darwen Football Club. They performed well in the Lancashire Combination with two 4th place finishes in their first two season back, followed by three consecutive 3rd places in 1923/24, 1924/25 and 1925/26.

Bob Jackson was one of Darwen's top players during this post war period but he was quickly snatched up by Football League side Bury in October 1922. As part of the deal, Bury visited Darwen at the Anchor Ground for a friendly match on 24th April 1923, which Darwen won 3-1. Jackson later went on to manage Portsmouth.

The club had not won anything since 1902, but silverware was not far away. On 18th November 1922, Darwen visited Accrington Stanley - who were, by then, playing in Football League Division 3 North - to play for the East Lancs Charity Shield and won 4-2 in front of a 6,000 crowd at Peel Park.

By this time, crowds of 4,000 and 5,000 - numbers that had not been seen in Darwen for some 40 years - had again become commonplace and the club was able to benefit from the increased revenue to gradually improve the ground.

In anticipation of the 1923/24 season, the *Lancashire Daily Post Football Annual* said of Darwen: *"Darwen's prospects for the season are distinctly good. A spacious grandstand on the westerly side of the Anchor Ground will add greatly to the comfort of the spectators."*

Darwen FC 1921/22 with Shield
Back: Proos, Wilson, Hardman, Murray, Suttie, Ellel
Front: Halt, Taylor, Birch, Snape, Williams, Stevenson
(source: Golden Jubilee Booklet/Mrs Merrick)

In the above photo, despite the poor picture quality, it is just possible to see part of the initial frame structure of one of the new stands in the background.

One year later, in 1924/25, the *Post* annual said: *"Though they still have a balance on the wrong side, Darwen's finances are better than was the case twelve months ago and the prospects for the club from every point are improved. Last season a large portion of the banking on one side of the ground was covered. On the other side of the field is a large stand which has now become the property of the club."*

In 1925, Darwen once again played Accrington Stanley for the East Lancs Charity Shield, this time over two legs on 16th and 28th April.

The first leg was away at Peel Park and Darwen's centre forward Livesey scored the only goal of the game after just 6 minutes to give the Darreners a big boost for the second leg.

The return match - played on a pitch that was ankle deep in mud in some areas - ended with a 1-0 win to Accrington Stanley meaning that extra time had to be played to decide the winners. Two periods of ten minutes each were played and, just as it seemed that the stalemate would remain, Accrington scored a vital with just two minutes left. As if that weren't enough Darwen scored with the very last kick of the game - a free kick by Hart - to level the aggregate scores once again. The goal was greeted by, according to the press report: *"such an outburst of enthusiasm that has not been seen on the Darwen ground for a very long time"*.

It was agreed that the Shield would be shared and each team received a set of medals.

For the first game of the 1925/26 season, played on 29th August, Darwen made a little bit of history by being the opponents for Clitheroe's first ever game in the Lancashire Combination.

More history was made that day as Jack Slater - who would become an important of the great 1930s side - made his debut for Darwen.

Over the course, of the season the club had actually made a profit for this first time since its reformation in 1920, although in those previous years a lot had been spent on rebuilding the ground.

The club was now in the "black" and had a ground to rival any in the Lancashire Combination. With a firm basis to build upon, Darwen Football Club slowly began to put together the foundations of a successful team, under the direction of captain and later manager Bert Proos, who had played with Blackburn Rovers alongside Bob Crompton and Arthur Cowell before the war.

It was not to happen overnight, however, and there were still a couple of rocky seasons to get through before the club finally hit upon the right combination of players.

In the 1926/27 season, Darwen had their first sniff of success in the highly rated Lancashire Junior Cup, reaching the semi final before losing 1-0 to Morecambe. But the league position was somewhat precarious as Darwen finished in 12th place - their lowest placing since the end of the war.

The following season Albert Leeming made his debut for the club and Darwen again reached the semi final of the Junior Cup. This time they hammered Morecambe 7-2 in the 3rd round but, once again, came unstuck in the semi-final, losing to Lancaster 3-1. Rather worryingly, the league form plummeted even further and they finished second from bottom of the Combination.

Towards the end of the 1927/28 season, Albert Robinson signed for the club from Fleetwood and the team was strengthened further during the summer with the arrival of former Fulham centre half Albert Pope who joined as player coach, George Shaw from Preston North End and Paddy Quigley from Accrington.

1928/29 Lancashire Junior Cup

Darwen only managed to finish in 11th place in the Combination in the 1928/29 season, although that was already a great improvement over the 19th place the previous year. Another area of improvement came in the Lancashire Junior Cup where they finally managed to reached the final at the third time of asking.

They beat Bacup 4-0 away after a replay in the second round before overcoming eventual Combination champions Chorley, with whom an intense local rivalry had built up over the years, 5-2 in the next round in front of 6,000 crowd 5-2.

The semi final was played in thick fog away at Ashton National who had several ex Football League players in their ranks. Darwen went 1-0 down early in the first half but equalised before half time. Then a George Shaw goal early in the secured a 2-1 win although, by then, the visibility was so bad that few of the travelling Darwen fans in the 3,700 crowd would have been able to see it.

The final was played at Preston North End's Deepdale ground on 12th January 1929 and Darwen's opponents were Lancaster Town who had appeared in the previous three finals and six times in all.

Darwen FC 1929 Cup Final Team at Deepdale
Back: Bishop, Slater, Jenkinson, Mulkeen, Richardson, Quigley, Leeming,
Proos/ Front: Robinson, Clarkson, Pape, Fry, Shaw, Botterill
(source: Slater Family)

The game was played in front of a healthy 9,000 crowd and remained balanced on a knife edge well into the second half. It was goalless at half time but Lancaster took the lead in the 72nd minute forcing Darwen to push forward looking for an equaliser.

George Shaw had aggravated an existing injury early in the game and so was not able to play to his full potential and Lancaster scored again with 6 minutes left on the clock

Darwen lost the match 2-0 on the day but, in doing so, gained some very useful experience of cup finals that would hold the team in good stead for the years that followed.

Season 1929-30

Hoping to build on the previous season's rather disappointing 11th place finish, Darwen FC announced that 9 first team players would be retained and that, despite attention from Manchester United, it was confirmed that goalkeeper Mulkeen would be staying with the club.

To add to the 9 first team players retained from last season several interesting signings were made at the start of the new campaign, including Clemmett - an inside left from Breightmet United and Wilson - an outside left formerly with Scottish First Division Side Cowdenbeath.

The season stated of well for Darwen with a succession of victories and the club experimented with different forward lines. On 31st August, they fought back from being 2-1 down away at Dick Kerrs at half time to win the match 4-2 with second half with goals from Shaw, Robinson and Gaskell.

On 17th September, a new frontline of Monks, Shaw and Clemmett ran riot against Lytham winning 7-0 after a slender 1-0 lead at half time and Clemmett was once again the star of the match on 5th October, scoring 3 goals as Darwen beat Great Harwood 8-1 in the Combination Cup.

On the first day of November, the team was further strengthened with a player who was to become very important over the next couple of season. Forward Bob Dale - brother of the Manchester United and, later, City defender - signed from the Manchester Amateur League.

Dale made an immediate impact by scoring on his league debut for the club the very next day in a 5-1 win over Barnoldswick Town, although Clemmett was man of the match once again with the other four goals.

Manchester Central were unbeaten in the league at that stage and Darwen were drawn to play them away in the Junior Cup.

Clemmett struck first and it looked as if Darwen were on their way to an unexpected victory until former Bolton legend Joe Smith scored a late equaliser for Manchester to force the replay. The Anchormen warmed up for the replay with a big home win over last season's Combination champions Chorley and then overcame Manchester by 3 goals to 2, Robinson scoring the winning goal just 5 minutes from time.

In the semi final they were drawn to play Morecambe at the Anchor Ground and, fielding an unchanged side, Darwen raced to a 3-0 lead by half time, doubtless aided by the fierce wind at their backs and a pitch that local newspaper reports described as a quagmire.

They added two more in the second half against the wind and the final score of 5-1 meant that Darwen had reached the final of the Lancashire Junior Cup for the second successive season - this time their opponents would be Horwich RMI.

Preparations for the final did not go well, however, on 21st December they slumped to a 6-0 league defeat away at Manchester Central and had to play part of the second half with 10 men, after losing Paddy Quigley with an injury. Then their home game against Atherton was abandoned because of bad weather after Darwen had raced to a 2-0 lead against the wind.

Furthermore, Darwen were then drawn to play Horwich - in the 3rd round of the Combination Cup as well. That game was played at the Anchor Ground on 2nd January and Darwen won 2-1 - both goals by Shaw, the deciding strike coming as a second half penalty.

Darwen fans might have expected that victory to boost their team's confidence for the big final that was, again, to be played at Deepdale. Unfortunately that was not to be the case and the day before the final, the news was announced that George Shaw would probably miss the big game with a knee injury

That meant that, from the previous season's cup final team, only Mulkeen, Jenkinson, Slater, Williamson, Quigley and Robinson remained.

Darwen FC 1930 Junior Cup Final Team
Back: Proos, Williamson, Jenkinson, Quigley, Mulkeen, Dawson, Slater, Bishop
Front: Robinson, Prest, Shaw, Clemmett, Wilson
(source: Blackburn with Darwen Library and Information Service)

The weather conditions for the final were not good and there was thin carpet of snow on the Deepdale turf. George Shaw was not fit and a last minute replacement - Harry Brogden a former Oxford Blue - was brought in up front.

As the game got underway, the Darwen team appeared to be showing signs of nerves. Horwich had much less of the play but the Darreners were unable to take the advantage in a goalless first half. In the end Horwich won the game 2-0 but most observers felt that this was more down to deficiencies in the Darwen team rather than any superiority on Horwich's part.

The local press report said; "*Darwen had much the better of the play throughout but met a fine goalkeeper and two snap goals gave Horwich the cup*"

Two days later Tommy Prest was sold to Burnley for £600. He had actually signed for Burnley some weeks beforehand but a special clause in the contract allowed him to carry on playing for Darwen until after the cup final appearance.

Darwen then played Horwich for an incredible third time in as many weeks when they travelled to meet the Railwaymen in a league game on 25th January. This time, there were no nerves and, after drawing 2-2 at half time, the Valley team came away with a vengeful 6-3 away win.

The following week, Darwen were due to entertain Manchester Central in the league and were able to gain some revenge for their earlier hammering in Manchester by inflicting Central's first league defeat of the season. They beat them 4-2 at the Anchor Ground, with Bob Dale weighing in with two important goals.

On 8th April there was a brief break from competitive action as the Anchor Ground hosted a benefit for Darwen's John Slater(pictured below). Little is recorded of how the game went but the *Northern Daily Telegraph* referred to it as: *"a well deserved tribute to the services he has rendered the club"*

On 14th April, Darwen beat Accrington Stanley Reserves 3-0 at home in the Semi final of the Combination Cup to reach their second cup final of the season. Shaw scored twice and Dale got the third but spectators observed that, such was Darwen's superiority, they might easily have scored 5.

Two days later, Darwen suffered their first home defeat for some 5 months losing 0-2 to eventual league champions Lancaster.

On 24th April, Darwen played Bacup at home in the final of the East Lancs Charity Shield, having beaten Rossendale in the semi final.

(Note: The format of this competition seems to have been changed around almost every season, depending on which teams wished to take part in it - as was the East Lancs Charity Cup which was now back to being played for among the senior clubs in the area such as Burnley and Blackburn. On this occasion, the shield was played as 2 semi finals and a final).

The first half was goalless and despite leading 1-0 and then 2-1, Darwen lost the match 4-2 with the closing stages of the being played in semi darkness.

Lancashire Combination Cup Final

Losing at home in the shield just a few days beforehand could not have been very good preparation for Darwen's 3rd final of the season, especially as they had to cram in 6 games in 10 days. The task was doubly daunting as the reds would have to play Prescot Cables away in Prescot in the final

The game was played on the evening of Monday 28th April and, working on the basis of the motto *"third time lucky"*, Darwen came out with all guns blazing.

Both sides had their chances but, as the first half wore on, Darwen took control. In the 40th minute Wilson took a corner quickly and Paddy Quigley headed into the net to give Darwen the lead.

73

Almost straight from the kick off, Darwen were back in the Prescot penalty area, as the *Northern Daily Telegraph* of the day describes: *"A crashing drive from Slater hit the underside of the crossbar but fell well into the net only to bounce back and with the referee not near enough, the Cables escaped."*

Prescot threw everything they could muster at the Darwen defence in the second half but Mulken *"did glorious deeds on two or three occasions"*. Darwens's second goal came from a nice bit of play by Quigley who *"did some marvellous things in the way of controlling the ball before it hit the ground"*. He picked out Shaw in some space who fired past the advancing Prescot goalkeeper.

The final score was 2-0 to Darwen and victory and captain Paddy Quigley was presented with the Cup. Interestingly enough, this was the same cup that Darwen had received in 1901/02 as champions of the Lancashire League.

In the league they finished 4th. But, after losing the Junior Cup final in January they had won 19 and lost only 5 of their 25 games - form which, had it been maintained throughout the season, would have given Darwen a higher finishing place in the Lancashire Combination table.

The team was more settled and only 28 players were used in the 38 league games. Mulkeen and Robinson played in all 51 league and cup matches and, of the 128 league and cup goals scored overall, 43 came from the boots of George Shaw.

Season 1930/31

Having won the Combination Cup the previous year, Darwen were keen to improve on their 4th place in the league.

The Blackburn Times of 16th August reported that the team would remain very much in place from last season, the only notable exception being goalkeeper Mulkeen who had moved to Kent for work reasons.

As the season got under way, centre forward Clemmett was transferred to Preston North End but any feeling of loss was soon forgotten, as, in early September, Darwen pulled off a huge coup by signing former Bolton Wanderers England international star Joe Smith (pictured above) from Manchester Central.

The inside left had spent 19 years in the Football League with Bolton, winning the FA Cup and making 5 appearances for his country.

A huge crowd was in attendance at the Anchor Ground on 9th September to witness Smith's debut for the Valley team. And they were not to be disappointed as they were treated to a 10-2 demolition of visiting Wigan Borough Reserves, with Dale and Shaw scoring 5 goals each.

Darwen set the early pace in the Lancashire Combination, notching up 11 points from a possible 12 in their first 6 games and they headed the league table by mid September. Then came the first defeat of the season - 2-1 at home to Dick Kerrs

On 13th December, Reginald Preedy - who had just months before only been playing junior district football in Clitheroe - was promoted from the reserve side to the first team and scored a hat-trick on his debut!

A typical 1930s view of Reg Preedy attacking the goal
(source: Blackburn with Darwen Library and Information Service)

Two weeks later, when Darwen beat Rochdale Reserves 12-1, Joe
Smith scored five of the goal but Preedy scored six more to bring his
total to 15 in just 5 games with onlookers suggesting that he was
"the next Johnny Ball".

However, such goal-scoring form did not go unnoticed and Burnley
quickly swooped to sign the promising 20 year old who had, by then,
added a third hat trick to his tally. But Preedy was still only
registered as an amateur with Darwen. His rise to prominence had
been so quick that he had not been offered better terms by the club
and, as such, he had to be released with no fee changing hands.

Darwen were unhappy as they had not been officially approached by
Burnley before they offered Preedy a contract and the move was
described in the club's records as a *"dirty low-down trick"*.

But the loss of Preedy did not stop the Darwen rollercoaster. After
the new year holiday games, Darwen were back up to second in the
Combination and a week later were top of the league on goal
average with two games in hand over second placed Dick Kerrs.

On 20th January, Fred Dawson was promoted from the reserves to the first team and he too scored a hat trick thus becoming the third Darwen debutant in that position to score a hat trick in the past two months.

East Lancs Charity Shield - An Unusual Game

On 17th February, Darwen entertained Clitheroe in the East Lancs Charity Shield at the Anchor Ground. The weather conditions were appalling with a strong icy wind and snow on the ground.

It was 1-1 at half time courtesy of a Shaw goal but, as the second half got underway, more snow began to fall. Darwen now had the advantage of a very strong gale behind them and Shaw scored two goals within 90 seconds of the restart.

It was so cold that the referee called the players off the field for a short time and when he brought them back out to restart the game, only 10 Darwen players re-emerged and seven from Clitheroe. Joe Smith added three more goals in the second half as, one by one, the remaining Clitheroe players succumbed to the cold and left the field.

By the time the referee abandoned the match with 8 minutes left to play, Darwen were leading 7-1 and Clitheroe only had four men left on the pitch. Rather than face a replay, Clitheroe scratched from the competition.

***

Back in the league, Darwen travelled the short distance to Peel Park, Accrington on 21st February to face the Stanley reserve - a ground on which they had not taken a single point for 6 years. The 2000 crowd witnessed a 1-1 draw which was a great morale booster to Darwen's championship drive.

A 5-1 defeat away at fellow title contender Prescot Cables was quickly avenged with a 3-0 home win three days later but Darwen's championship hopes would have to depend on other results going their way as well.

Darwen virtually assured themselves of the league title with a resounding 8-0 win over Great Harwood, learning at the same time that Prescot Cables had lost their match the same day.

Combination Cup

Darwen opened their defence of the cup with a 5-1 win over Great Harwood in which Joe Smith scored 3 goals.

In the next round they faced Clitheroe in a match that they won 4-2 after having been 2-1 down at half time. Fred Dawson scored the equaliser and the all important third goal.

The semi final against Chorley was a hard fought affair and Darwen lost Paddy Quigley after just 10 minutes through injury and were reduced to only four forwards for the rest of the game. Chorley were leading 1-0 as the final minutes ticked away but Joe Smith scored a lat minute equaliser to earn Darwen a replay.

A 5,000 crowd was present on 20th April at Chorley's Victory Park to watch the replay. This time a fully fit Darwen side made light work of the opposition winning 3-1 with goal from Smith (2) and Robinson.

The final was played on 28th April faced Southport Reserves at Haigh Avenue in the final before a 3,500 crowd. This was essentially an away game at Southport's home ground, so the fact that Darwen won by such a great margin is a great credit to the team. Joe Smith scored two first half goals and Shaw added two more in the second half to secure a 4-0 win.

In the Charity Shield, Darwen once again faced Bacup Borough in the final. Dawson missed a penalty before half time by which time Bacup had taken a 2-0 lead. Luckily for the Darreners, Bob Dale pulled two goals back late in the second half to level the game with 9 minutes to go.

In the replay at the Anchor Ground Dale again scored twice in a 2-0 win that secured Darwen their third trophy of the season.

Darwen's 1930/31 Treble Winning Team
Proos, Slater, Bennett, Smith, Rowlands, Dawson, Leeming, J Bishop
Richardson, Robinson, Quigley, J Smith, Preedy, Dale, Shaw, Jenkinson
Combination Cup, Charity Shield and Combination Trophy
(source: Nora Thompson)

A triumphant return to Darwen with the three trophies
(source: Nora Thompson)

The final Lancashire Combination game of the season was played away at Clitheroe on 2nd May 1931 but, in reality, it was more of a carnival than a football match as Darwen had already secured the league title, cup and shield. Many hundreds of Darwen fans travelled to the game and the Darwen band played on the pitch beforehand and at half time.

For the record, the game ended in a 1-1 draw. George Shaw scored a second half penalty for Darwen to level the score but the game was of secondary importance to the travelling contingent that day. All three trophies were on display in the grandstand throughout the match decorated in Darwen's colours and a formal presentation was made after the game by the Lancashire Combination president TP Campbell.

Looking back over a great season, the club board was later to comment that the *"success resulted in a greatly improved financial position of which many a 3rd Division team would be glad".*

Focus on Paddy Quigley (From a special *Northern Daily Telegraph* article)

Patrick Quigley was born in Londonderry on 21st July 1898. His mother did not approve of football, calling it a "murtherous game", but, despite his parents' disapproval, he played for several local junior football teams and was selected to play for Ireland in a junior international match against Scotland.

The team that he played for - Derry Distillery - once went a whole season without defeat but then the sectarian troubles flared in that part of Ireland and all football was suspended.

Paddy was by then working as a civil servant and, as luck would have it, he was offered a transfer to a government post in Accrington with the Post Office. He moved to Lancashire, applied for a trial with Accrington Stanley and was signed as a player in 1921.

Quigley could have easily played at a higher level of football. He hadn't been at Accrington very long when Preston North End showed an interest in signing him. He played a couple of times for them but found that the stringent training requirements and long distances to matches across the country did not fit in with his job at the Post Office. He chose not to stay, citing the greater long term security that his job offered him and, in 1928, signed for Darwen.

"The Critic" - a columnist in the early 1930s - describes the player as having *"those personal qualities which have won him the wholesome respect of those with whom he comes in close contact"* and that he was always *"above the class represented by Lancashire Combination football."*

He continues to say that *"Paddy is imbued with the finest spirit of the game"*, is *"a loyal servant to the Darwen club"* and *"an ideal comrade"* with *"a frank admiration for the pleasing qualities in others"*, often known to *"speak admiringly of opponents"*.

Season 1931/32

The optimism for the new season following the treble success was somewhat overshadowed by the fact that the previous season's leading light and goal machine Joe Smith had decided to hang up his boots and retire from playing. He went on to successfully manage Blackpool for 23 years winning the FA Cup in the famous "Matthews Final" of 1953.

With Frank Dawson being snatched up by Manchester United, Darwen would have to rely on Bob Dale and Paddy Quigley for their goals this time around. Luckily for the club, if not the player, Reg Preedy had not been able to make a go of it at Burnley and only stayed for 6 weeks before returning to Darwen for the final months of the treble campaign.

Initially it was the various cup competitions that provided the most interest to the Darwen public. On 7th November Darwen played Horwich RMI away in the Junior Cup. This was the team that had beaten them in the final in 1929/30 but this time Darwen came away with a 9-0 win - Reg Preedy scoring 6.

In the FA Cup, they had successfully negotiated the various qualifying rounds beating Burscough, Dick Kerrs, Lytham and Prescot Cables to reach the first round proper of the competition for the first time since they moved to the Anchor Ground in 1899.

The opponents for the big cup tie were Peterborough and Fletton United for the Southern League who, as things turned out, were easily beaten with 2 goals from Dale, 1 from Quigley and 1 from half back Norman Crompton, who had joined Darwen from Horwich earlier in the season.

Darwen were drawn against Chester City - then one of the top teams in the 3rd Division North - in the second round but had an anxious wait after Peterborough complained to the FA that Darwen had used an ineligible player in goalkeeper Rowlands.

Luckily for the reds, the protest was dismissed and, on 12th December, they faced the Division 3 North leaders at the Anchor Ground in what was the club's biggest test in years.

The game attracted a record 6,500 crowd and Bert Proos jr, who saw the match, recalls: *"it was absolutely packed. They couldn't possibly get another soul on that ground."*

Things got off to a bad start when Darwen full back Murray scored an own goal but Darwen kept their heads and refused to give in to this early set back. In what has since been described as *"one of the best ever games to be seen at the Anchor Ground"*, Reg Preedy scored twice to clinch the win for the Darreners.

To celebrate the great victory, a rhyme sprung up around Darwen. Former club secretary Jack Haworth quotes it as:

"There are people in sleepy Chester
Bemoan they have not won
There's a ground by the Darwen river
On which they scored but one
And there's Robinson Preedy Quigley
Who tell how this deed was done..!"

The draw for the third round was keenly awaited and Darwen could not have been given a bigger pairing and a sterner test - they were drawn to play the mighty Arsenal at Highbury!

In the run up to the game there was a lot of media interest, not just locally but nationally as well.

James Briggs, Darwen's team manager, told the *Darwen News* in an exhibition of pre-match psychology that even Sir Alex Ferguson would be proud of: *"there is not a better lot of fighters anywhere than our men. If it is a draw at Highbury until the last 20 minutes, Darwen will win. Our team is full of beans. They will play every one of the 90 minutes and still be fresh and the heavier the ground the better we shall like it."*

Darwen players demonstrating an early form of product endorsement when they were presented with new overalls by the Liverpool company *John Peck & Co (source: Slater Family).*

The *Northern Daily Telegraph* of the time listed the occupations of the players who were selected to play in the big match:

Rowlands: Unemployed, Heaton Moor
Murray: Cotton spinner, Heywood
Jenkinson: Cotton mill operative, Barnoldswick
Slater: Mill operative, Rishton
Crompton: Unemployed, Farnworth
Leeming: Motor body builder, Preston
Robinson: Fish docker, Fleetwood
Dale: Labourer, Manchester
Preedy: Cotton mill operative, Clitheroe
Quigley: Post Office worker, Accrington
Shaw: Motor driver, Chorley

By today's standards the distances that these players had to travel for training and games may not seem too far but in the 1930s they represented a much greater obstacle to overcome. Quite often work commitments made it hard for the players to get to weekly training sessions.

In the run up to the biggest game of their lives, the Darwen players could not sit back and soak up the atmosphere. They had to work during the week.

"No salt sea air, brine baths or restful recreation has taken part in their preparation. Work is the training the Darwen men thrive on. "

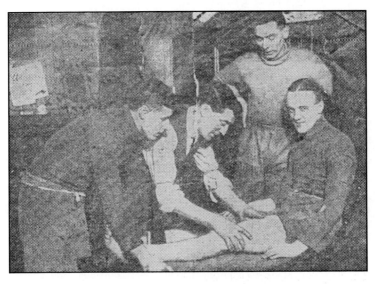

Reg Preedy receiving massage from Proos
while Slater and Smith look on
(source: Slater Family)

But the spirit in the Darwen camp was terrific. Even Jack Slater who had not been selected to play and would only accompany the team down as a reserve travelled in for the latter part of the midweek training session that his working hours allowed him to manage.

Punchball training for Smith, Shaw and Slater
(source: Nora Thompson)

The *Telegraph* reporter watched him *"running cheerfully around the pitch dark water soaked ground. Later he punched a ball, was rubbed down and had a bath. That was all the training his work had left him time for"*.

Albert Leeming was luckier, his working hours allowed him the time to go and have electro massage, radiant heat and sun ray treatment at the hands of Joe Bishop, the club's masseur who had been with the club since the early 1920s.

Joe Bishop's daughter, Nora Thompson - now in her 80s - remembers clearly the days when the players would walk down to the Bishop house at the bottom of Avondale Road from the Anchor Ground on training nights when they needed treatment. But, as her father could only treat one at a time, the others would play darts and table tennis with her and her friends while they were waiting for their turn on the massage table.

FRIDAY, JANUARY 8th, 1931.

10-30 a.m.   Meet at Station Garage.

10-56 a.m.   Train Departs for Euston, London. Lunch en route.

3-55 p.m.   Arrive Euston.   Taxis to Strand Palace and Regent Palace Hotels.

6-0 p.m.   Dinner at the Strand Palace Hotel.

7-30 p.m.   Leave for Saville Theatre.   "For the Love of Mike."

SATURDAY, JANUARY 9th, 1932.

8-45 a.m.   Breakfast.

9-45 a.m.   Coach to House of Commons, to be received by the Rt. Hon. Sir Herbert Samuel, G.C.B., G.B.E., M.P.

11-30 a.m.   Light Luncheon, Strand Palace Hotel.

12-30 p.m.   Coach to Highbury.

4-45 p.m.   Return from Highbury to Strand Palace Hotel.

6-0 p.m.   Dinner.

7-40 p.m.   Leave for Winter Gardens.   "Walk this Way."

SUNDAY, JANUARY 10th, 1932.

9-0 a.m.   Breakfast.   Morning at leisure.

11-40 a.m.   Leave for Euston by Taxi.

12-10 p.m.   Train leaves for Darwen.   Lunch en route.

6-34 p.m.   Arrive Darwen.

The Players and Directors are the Guests of the Rt. Hon. Sir Herbert Samuel, G.C.B., G.B.E., M.P., at the Dinner on Saturday and afterwards at the Winter Gardens Theatre.

YOUR strict attention to this Programme will add to the success of the arrangements.

Itinerary for trip to London
(source: Slater Family)

PROGRAMME

for the visit of the

Darwen Football Club (1922) Ltd.

to LONDON for the

ARSENAL v. DARWEN

MATCH

in the THIRD ROUND, F.A. CUP, on

SATURDAY, JANUARY 9th, 1932.

OFFICIALS.

Ald. GEORGE PICKUP, J.P., C.C., PRESIDENT.
Mr. HARRY HARWOOD, CHAIRMAN.
Mr. JOHN WOOD, VICE-CHAIRMAN.
Mr. THOMAS B. WOOD.
Mr. HERBERT HACKING.
Mr. ALBERT HORNBY.
Mr. HOUGHTON AINSWORTH.
Mr. WILLIAM DUXBURY.
Mr. JAMES H. BRIGGS.
Mr. JOSEPH S. ENTWISTLE.
Mr. JOHN C. RILEY.

SECRETARY, ELLIS MARSDEN, A.I.S.A.
Registered Office,
BELGRAVE CHAMBERS, DARWEN.

9th January 1932 - The Arsenal Game

As it was such a special occasion, the Darwen players and officials travelled down to London the day before the game and a large crowd congregated at Darwen station to see them off.

Upon arrival in London, the party were welcomed at the House of Commons by were shown round by Sir Herbert Samuel MP who was Darwen MP and Home Secretary at the time.

They stayed overnight at a luxury hotel and Bert Proos - son of the Darwen trainer - remembers admiring the shining silverware in the hotel restaurant: *"the big chief of the hotel said to me if you beat Arsenal tomorrow, you can take all those cups off the display back to Darwen with you..."*

Bert was Darwen's mascot and always ran on to the pitch in the club colours before the game and the Arsenal game was no exception. In those days the use of mascots was by no means a common occurrence - even *The Times* remarked upon his presence: *"a great crowd of over 35,000 enjoyed every moment from the time a little nipper came out with the Darwen team in the club colours and kicked the ball through the goal."*

The Arsenal team that day was packed with top stars and internationals but manager Herbert Chapman had done Darwen the courtesy of telling his team not to go easy but to go for as many goals as they could.

Darwen, however, showed lots of tenacity and, according to *The Times*, even started off the better team in *"the first two minutes of the match during which Darwen attacked the Arsenal goal and had a shot and kept Arsenal on the defensive, even with a strong wind at their backs...."*

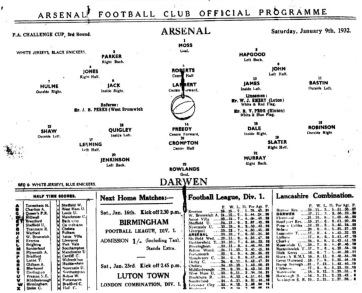

Matchday programme for the big game
(source: Slater Family)

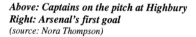

Above: Captains on the pitch at Highbury
Right: Arsenal's first goal
(*source: Nora Thompson*)

But, despite this early flourish there was to be little doubt about the result and it was 8-0 to the Gunners by half time.

Bert Proos remembers the match with great fondness: "*Of course, up against such players as Alec James, Tom Parker, Cliff Bastin - who was a wizard on the wing for England - and the like, what chance did Darwen have..? When I came off the field, I went into the dressing room. My dad came in after maybe 10 minutes or a quarter of an hour and he said "it's two - nothing" and I naively asked him: "who to...?"*

The match finished 11-1 to Arsenal but Darwen tried their best throughout and acquitted themselves well against the reigning league champions and eventual cup finalists. *The Times* reported that "*Darwen did a good deal of attacking and forced quite a few corners and from one Dale, the inside right and their best forward, scored.*"

Bob Dale's historic goal for the minnows from Lancashire was Darwen's 100th goal of the season.

Despite the scoreline, the Darwen team were the big celebrities in London that night.

Bert Proos said: *"On the Saturday night, we were invited to go up to the theatre on Shaftesbury Avenue and Gracie Fields was there. We went round the back to see her and she sat me on her knee and gave me a kiss."*

The team were invited up onto the stage after the performance of *"Walk This Way"* and given a rousing reception by the audience.

The following day, the team returned from London and were greeted by over 2,000 fans who had braved the pouring rain to welcome their returning heroes at Darwen station.

***

Following the game at Arsenal, Rowlands, the amateur goalkeeper, was signed by Manchester United and, once again, the records reveal that the club was *"never consulted and gain no recompense"*.

Undeterred by this and, now, no longer having to contend with the distractions of the FA Cup, Darwen moved up to the top of the Lancashire Combination after a 2-0 win over leaders Nelson who, only the previous season had been playing in the Football League.

At the beginning of April, the Darreners lost their first league game for 6 months and it couldn't have been worse as the 2-1 defeat came at the hands of fellow title contenders Prescot Cables. Luckily Prescott then went on to drop a vital point away at Accrington and confirmed that the Lancashire Combination championship would go to Darwen for the second successive season.

Combination Cup

On 26th April Darwen beat Barnoldswick in the semi-final of the Combination Cup to reach the final for the third year in succession. However, the choice of venue for the final caused a bit of a stir.

Darwen discovered that they would have to play Fleetwood away on their own ground and, as club secretary Ellis Marsden commented: *"the Fleetwood ground is so small, it gives the home club a big advantage"*.

The Darwen club thought that home advantage should have been decided by the toss of a coin, as had been the case on previous occasions, but the cup committee countered with the argument that the venue had been chosen before the finalists were known.

So it was a rather half hearted Darwen side that travelled to Fleetwood on 3rd May and lost the final 5-0 in front of a crowd of 5,900 - a record for the cup at that stage. This was their worst defeat (excluding the Arsenal game) for some 29 months.

The final home game of the season was just two days later on 5th May and the Combination championship trophy was presented after the game. However the occasion was marred as the crowd booed the league officials because of their intransigence over the cup final venue.

Darwen FC 1931/32 - Champions Again
Proos, Smith, Slater, Murray, Rowlands, Crompton, Quigley, Bishop
Robinson, Jenkinson, Preedy, Dale, Leeming, Shaw
(source: Nora Thompson)

92

4th August 1932 - Opening of the New Stand

Darwen's share of the £2.468 gate money from the FA Cup game at Arsenal was enough to enable them to build a new covered stand behind the goal at the "Darwen End".

According to the official programme for the grand opening (shown below) the steel structure was 74 yards by 8 yards and would provide accommodation for 3,000 people. Mention was also made of the generosity of the supporters' club in the venture.

The stand was officially opened by Darwen captain Paddy Quigley and guests of honour for the occasion were the mayor of Darwen - Cllr W Jepson - and the "Cotton Queen of Britain", Miss Marjorie Knowles who was pretty much the Kate Moss of her day.

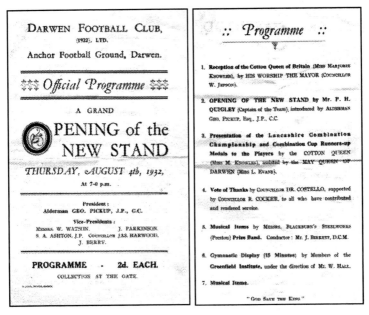

Programme for the Grand Opening
(source: Slater Family)

Mid 1930s view of ground showing the new "Arsenal" stand
(source: Blackburn with Darwen Library & Information Service)

1932/33 - Lancashire Junior Cup

The following season, Darwen were unable to continue their dominance of the Lancashire Combination and could only manage a 4th place finish. However, they did, finally, win the Lancashire Junior Cup in the 1933 final, played at Deepdale.

The game, played on 1st May, saw them pitted against Lancaster and the Darwen team that day was: Vickers (gk), Murray, Jenkinson, Slater, Summers, Leming, Edwards, Cooper, Whitty, Preedy and Quigley.

The match finished goalless and was replayed 4 days later, again at Deepdale. On this occasion there was no stopping Darwen and they ran away with the match, wining 5-0. George Shaw, who had missed the first game, scored twice and the other goals came from Cooper, Preedy and Quigley.

After that 1933 cup win, the great Darwen team that had won the title twice in a row gradually began to split up. Some of the players came to the end of their careers while the younger ones, who had been put in the spotlight by the recent successes, were snatched up by other clubs.

The crowds that had, in recent years, flocked to the Anchor Ground had got used to seeing a winning team. Once that team stopped winning, the crowds stopped coming. The gate revenue fell, the club struggled financially and this time around, there were no were no healthy FA Cup runs to help fill the coffers.

In 1932/33, Darwen battled through two hard fought replays with local rivals Chorley to get through to the FA Cup 1st round. They were drawn away at 3rd Division side Halifax but didn't make much of a showing, losing 2-0.

The following season they once again got through to the 1st round of the FA Cup and once again drew 3rd Division opposition.

The opponents were Gateshead who, ironically, at the time were in an even worse financial state than Darwen. The game, played before a huge 7,700 crowd at Redheugh Park was a bruising encounter and ended in a 5-2 mauling for Darwen. George Shaw got injured and, in his absence, Darwen flattered going into the last half of the league season, while the gate money and the promise of a bigger tie in the next round of the cup was just enough to save Gateshead from bankruptcy.

On two occasions during the mid 30s - in 1933 and 1934 - Darwen tried unsuccessfully to join the Cheshire League. Many of the Lancashire Combination's top clubs had transferred across and it was thought that such a move would bring more attractive opposition to Darwen, along with bigger crowds.

On both occasions they were unsuccessful in the voting ballots and had to carry on battling away in the Lancashire Combination.

In May 1934, both Darwen's star full backs Maurice Reeday and Arthur Grimes transferred to Blackpool for no fee.

The two players were out of contract at Darwen but had been placed on their retained list. However, as they had not been re-signed by Darwen at the time of Blackpool's approach, they had to be released without the fee that they would undoubtedly otherwise have commanded. This was not the first time that Darwen had lost a valuable player for no fee and would not be the last.

Maurice Reeday
(source: Blackburn with Darwen
Library & Information Service)

Reeday joined Accrington Stanley from Blackpool in 1936 and then moved to Leicester City for a four figure sum in 1937. During his time at Leicester, Reeday played three times against the legendary Stanley Matthews.

Leicester played Matthews' Stoke City three times in quick succession - once in the league and then in an FA Cup tie and replay - and Reeday kept the star centre forward off the scoresheet on each occasion.

The Daily Mirror serialised Mathhews' biography in 1961. Sir Stanley himself takes up the story: "*I had not even heard of Reeday up to that league game. In fact I did not know his name until after the game when I grabbed a programme anxious to find the name of my tormentor*

"*I found my early attempts to get round him failed. I went inside left. Mister Reeday was there again to take the ball off me. Eventually fed up with failure, I said: " haven't you got as home to go to?" He grinned and replied; "Yes, but it won't blow away before the game's finished."*

Unfortunately, the war deprived Reeday of what would have been his best years in first class football. On the outbreak of war he took a job in Accrington and played for the Howard and Bulloughs works team.

When the Stanley team started up again he played for them but suffered a knee injury which put him out for some time. In later years he played again for Darwen and also Nelson.

Commenting on how he managed to contain Matthews, the Darwen cobbler told the Darwen Advertiser: "*I never left Stanley very far and didn't give him much to work in. He needs more attention than most wingers but I never let him get the ball at his feet with a clear run.*"

Speaking recently about the Darwen team of the early 1930s, Bert Proos jnr recalls that Albert Robinson (outside right) used to work on the docks at Fleetwood and would often go to the Proos house for lunch on matchdays (the Bishop house as well, apparently) and "*he would always bring plenty of fish with him*". Bert Proos remembers him as "*a wizard on the right wing - today he would have been Premiership material.*"

George Shaw (outside left) came from Chorley and would always come by motorbike, which he always left in the Proos back garden as they lived close to the Anchor Ground at that time.

Paddy Quigley worked in the Post Office at Accrington. He was an Irish amateur international and had previously played for Accrington when Bert Proos senior had been playing for Darwen: "*a great pal of my dad's... many hard tackles between them.*"

Vic the gateman now still loyal to the club in his 80s, recalls watching the 1930s team as a young lad. He also has fond memories of Paddy Quigley: "*He never got booked or sent off but if someone got to him, he'd stand on their foot when there was a corner so they couldn't jump..!*"

Of star centre forward Reg Preedy, Vic says: "*He would come out onto the pitch looking immaculate - clean and tidy shirt and shorts, slicked back hair in perfect condition and he always left the field looking exactly the same after the game!!!*".

The story goes that, Arsenal Football Club were so impressed by the Darwen's show of sportsmanship when they played them in the 1932 FA Cup that they later presented them with a set of their own red and white playing colours.

The Darwen club then adopted those colours as their own and, with the exception of the 1970s, have worn red and white ever since. The above picture, supplied by Nora Thompson, dates from 1937 and shows the Darwen team in the *"Arsenal strip"*.

By 1935/36, Darwen were well and truly on the slippery slope down the Lancashire Combination table. They had not been able to recreate the halcyon days of the early 30s and a 4th and 5th place finish was followed this time around by 8th..

The team made an interesting signing in 1935 when Darwen had one of the first black players to play football in England - a West Indian player called Alf Charles who also played cricket for Nelson. The season also saw 17 year old Darwen "wonder boy" George Holden snapped up by Arsenal.

In November, Darwen they visited Scarborough in the FA Cup, hopeful that a good cup run could help ease the club's financial plight. Unfortunately, they lost 2-0 but reports say that Darwen should have had 2 penalties.

By now, club finances were at a very low ebb and a public appeal as made for donations to keep the team going. Only £50 was forthcoming.

The 1936/37 season saw ex England international left half back and former FA Cup winner Tom Johnson sign from Liverpool. He was joined by other big name arrivals such as Aussie Campbell from Blackburn Rovers and Matthew Johnson from Rochdale

In a season that saw Reg Preedy make his 300th appearance for the club, Darwen finished in their highest league position since the 1932 championship win, ending up in 3rd place..

They also rounded off the season with some silverware, or at least a share of it. Since the back to back championship wins, Darwen had found themselves invited back into the Lancashire Senior Cup for a couple of seasons, although they made little impression.

They had also been receiving regular beatings at the hands of Division 3 side Accrington Stanley in the Charity Shield so when Darwen were paired with Accrington again in the final of the East Lancs Charity Cup in April 1937, the likely outcome seemed easy to predict

The match was played at the Anchor Ground on 28th April 1937 and, at the end of 90 minutes, remained goalless. It had previously been announced that in the event of a draw there would be a replay at Peel park a few days later but prior to that, the fans were expecting extra time and a chance to find a winner on the day.

The two teams left the pitch and had a conference. The crowd began booing and jeering once it became clear that the players were not coming back out to play.

The officials of the two clubs then decided to dispense with the replay all together and share the trophy between them. That didn't go down well with the expectant fans either but the ensuing noisy demonstration did noting to change the minds of the two sets of officials and thus Darwen received one half share of a senior trophy.

1937/38 started badly for Darwen and they did not win until the 6th game of the season. Despite good new signings in Alec Finney, the former Bolton left back, Peter Vause from Blackburn and Joe Read - an outside right from Morecambe, Darwen dropped 9 points from a possible 18.

They had a good performance at South Liverpool in the FA Cup drawing 0-0 away but, in the replay on the following Tuesday, were down to 10 men after 10 minutes after an injury to full back King. They eventually lost the game 6-2.

In the league, Darwen suffered a heavy 10-1 defeat at South Liverpool. The Darwen goalkeeper Ingham hit his head against the post while making a diving save early in the first half. He played the rest of the game with concussion and had to say in hospital in Liverpool afterwards. He later said that he had no recollection whatsoever of any of the 10 goals that whizzed past him.

In the earlier part of the season, there had even been cautious talk of Darwen possibly winning the championship again but the team struggled with injuries throughout the season and, in the event, were lucky to finish in 7th place in the Combination.

The 1938/39 season started, once again, with high hopes but these were soon dashed as Darwen lost 3 of their first 4 home games in the League.

Goals were already a problem, 2 centre forwards were on the injured list - including Reg Preedy - and the situation was not helped when Peter Vause, who had only joined the club the season before, moved to Blackpool on 1st October.

In mid December 1938, the whole of Darwen's footballing public was shocked to learn that, after 7 years with the club, top goalscorer Reg Preedy had signed for Rossendale. In 327 games for Darwen he had scored a remarkable 334 goals. His departure left George Shaw as the only player still with the club to have played in the famous Arsenal match.

By a strange quirk of fate, Darwen had no home fixture between October and December 1938 and the club finances suffered badly through having no money through the gate. Then, in January, Bert Proos snr resigned as trainer after 12 years in the job. He had initially joined the club as a player in the 1911-12 season and played until 1927.

In October, Clifford Chatburn was signed from Burnley to solve the goal scoring problem and looked likely to be the *"next Reg Preedy"*. He scored 46 goals from the time he joined until the end of the season, including 5 on two occasions. Despite his efforts, the team was in decline. Darwen finished in 13th place in the league - their lowest finish since 1928.

The intervention of the Second World War mean that no-one will ever know if Chatburn would have been the next Preedy.

It also came at a time when the club was, once again, struggling desperately to survive and, having somehow managed to keep afloat, Darwen Football Club shut up shop for the duration of hostilities.

Chapter Four
Post War to Post Modern

The 1940s

Before the war, Darwen Football Club had stumbled from one financial crisis to another. Even during the war years when they were not playing, the club encountered bad luck as, in the hard winter of 1941, the west stand was wrecked by high winds.

It was only down to the generosity of a few friends and the timely arrival of a transfer fee from Burnley for Harry Jackson that the club was able to start up again after the war. Benny Pomfret was one of the few members of the pre-war side to return to playing action as the club rejoined the Lancashire Combination for the 1945/46 season.

Another player to feature in Darwen's first post-war campaign was inside right Ron Parry. He first played for Darwen in a testimonial match at the beginning of that season having been invited along by Jimmy Harrison, a former Leicester City and Hibernian centre forward, who he knew from Chorley and, after the game, he was invited to sign for Darwen.

After only 6 or 7 matches with the Peaceful Valley side, Parry was offered the chance to play for Blackpool in the Central League, which he accepted like a shot.

> **Photo at top of page: Ron Parry & Don Crispin**
> *By the refreshment shop on the corner of the Anchor Ground*
> *(source: Ron Parry)*

Before he moved on, however, he had a memorable game in the FA Cup as he recalls:

"I always remember in about my third match for Darwen we played in the FA Cup qualifying round against Skelmersdale. They were a Liverpool Combination side - very good team - and they came and got a draw at Darwen. Then we played them at Skelmersdale on the Wednesday night.

Skelmersdale had signed a full back from Preston called Gillimore. He was a very hard man - he let you know he was there!

We were playing extra time - it was dark then - we'd kicked off at 2.15 - there were no floodlights, of course, this ball came across and, it dropped to me and I stood on it. I heard this lad at the back say "he's mine, he's mine!" So I just back heeled it and the ball went straight into the corner of the net.

I remember Harry Harwood came over to me and gave me a good handshake because it was good money to the club in those days to progress in the FA Cup.

In the next round of the Cup, Darwen were drawn at old rivals Chorley but Ron Parry didn't play as he decided the night before the game that he wanted to go and join Blackpool instead. Ironically, he later played for Chorley in their 1948/49 Lancashire Combination winning season.

The team was strengthened mid way through the campaign with the signing of tricky outside left George Golden, who had previously played with Dundee and Southampton.

In a topsy-turvy league consisting of just 12 teams, Darwen finished in 5th place.

As things continued to get back to normal after the end of the war, the Lancashire Combination was extended to 22 teams for the 1946/47 season but Darwen could only manage 18th place.

Centre forward Chadwick still managed 30 league and cup goals and scored 4 in one match on two occasions.

Arthur Cowell, son of the Blackburn Rovers full back, appeared for Darwen and went on to be a prolific goalscorer both for them and for Nelson in the Lancashire Combination.

The following season was another one of disappointment, although the league finish was better. Darwen had a better defensive record and Arthur Cowell scored 30 goals during the course of the season. On 13th March 1948 Darwen signed right back Alf Pope from Blackpool. Ron Parry remembers that Pope played for Blackpool during the war while he was in the RAF. He also had a spell with Hearts in Scotland and went on to play over 100 times for Darwen.

Arthur Cowell (left)
and Alf Pope (right)
(source: Bob Eccles)

Darwen team (left) at the opening of
Morecambe's Christie Park
(source: Ron Parry)

Also in March 1948 Darwen signed left back Peter Barton - "*a good partner for Pope*" the press observed at the time. Barton had also been with Blackpool but Ron Parry recalls that he did not have the best of times there: "*A grand lad, Peter Barton - a belting bloke! He played in Blackpool's first team against Middlesbrough in the Cup - but they lost and blamed it on him*"

The Darwen team was strengthened for the 1948/49 season with the arrival of Jack Hughes, former Blackburn Rovers' Welsh international goalkeeper, and Ron Matthews, inside right brother of the more famous Stanley Matthews.

While league performances were good, the Reds' best chance of success looked to be the Lancashire Junior Cup as they beat Morecambe 4-2 in the semi final to reach the final for the first time since 1932.

Their opponents in the final were Barrow Reserves and, as Darwen had already taken maximum points from their two meetings with the Furness club in the Lancashire Combination, they must have been confident.

They had won 3-0 at Holker Street on 18th December and then did the double a week later when, on Christmas Day 1948, they beat Barrow 7-3. with goals from Strachan (3), Matthews (2), Cowell, Palmer and Wolstenholme.

The final was played on 12th May 1949 at Ewood Park in front of a 10,000 crowd and finished goalless although it was reported afterwards that the Barrow side had included a few members of their first team.

The replay was staged at Morecambe and the score was 1-1 at the end of normal time with Arthur Cowell having scored for Darwen. Unfortunately, the Barrow team scored twice without reply in extra time to take the cup with a 3-1 scoreline.

Darwen finished 5th in the Lancashire Combination that season, winning 21 of their 42 league games - their best placing since 1937 - but this proved to be a hard act to follow.

For the 1949 /50 season, Darwen could boast three ex internationals in the team with Hughes, Albert Geldard (ex Everton and England) and Ray Westwood (former Bolton and England).

Despite such high profile players, Darwen struggled in the league and could only manage 17th in the table. This form continued for the next two seasons with finishes of 15th and 16th and this lack of success saw crowd figures drop dramatically.

Apart from a brief upswing in 1952/53 when they finished 3rd and 1953/54 when they finished 5th, Darwen Football Club slipped back into the mid table mediocrity that had been on the cards ever since the break up of the great team of the early 1930s.

Golden Jubilee

In 1951, Darwen Football Club celebrated 50 years at the Anchor Ground by issuing a 32 page Golden Jubilee Souvenir Handbook.

Quite why they decided to do this in 1951 rather than 1949 is not made clear - not even within the booklet, although there is mention of Darwen having *"moved to the Anchor in 1900"*, which only serves to further confuse.

The book was put together by George H Hunt - Hon. Football Club Secretary - and Mervyn Martin - Hon Secretary of the Social Section - with the help of Alderman Knowles who had been a member of the board at the time of the move from Barley Bank, so one might expect him to know when the move actually took place.

The Anchor Ground in 1951 (see photo opposite)

By comparing this view with pictures of the main stand from the 1930s, it is possible to see how it looked after it had been damaged by heavy winds in the 1940s.

The booklet pays homage to "some of the stars who have worn the Darwen jersey" as are listed here. Some of these players are mentioned elsewhere in this book and some are not.

SOME OF THE STAR PLAYERS WHO HAVE WORN THE DARWEN JERSEY

Joe Smith.—The present Blackpool chief and former Bolton Wanderers and England centre-forward.

Alec. Finney.—Another famous Bolton player who ended his career with Darwen.

Bob Jackson.—Now manager of Portsmouth. Played for Darwen before moving on to Everton and Sheffield United.

Tom Johnson.—Inside-forward and England player. The third man in that famous inside trio that was the idol of Everton, namely, Dunn, Dean, and Johnson.

Alec Reid.—Another inside-forward. Made his name with Preston North End.

" Aussie " Campbell.—The famous England half-back. Played for Blackburn Rovers and Huddersfield prior to joining Darwen.

Harry Jackson.—Centre-forward. Began his career with Darwen in 1938. But for the war might well have developed into one of the best in the land. His clubs include Burnley, Preston, Manchester City and the Rovers.

Jack Hughes.—Welsh international goalkeeper, and one of the most reliable custodians ever to turn out for Darwen.

Albert Geldard.—Bolton Wanderers and England winger. Tried to stage a come-back with our club two seasons ago, but anno domini proved too much.

" Ray " Westwood.—Yet another Bolton player to end his playing career with the " Red and Whites," renowned for his deceptive swerve and strong left foot shot.

" Johnny " Ball.—A strong and fast centre-forward who left Darwen for Manchester United. Later moved on to Sheffield Wednesday.

Alf. Pope.—Great-hearted full-back. A real ninety minutes' player. Formerly captained Blackpool.

Maurice Reeday.—Darwen born and one of the most accomplished full-backs ever to play for our club. Stanley Matthews, in his memoirs, stated that Maurice was the only back he could never beat. Played for Blackpool, Accrington, and Leicester City before ending his playing career with his first love at the Anchor.

Albert Pape.—Centre-half and captain of Darwen in the mid-thirties. Was with Manchester United before joining our club.

Football In The 1950s

LOCAL FOOTBALL GALLERY

DARWEN F.C.—Back, left to right: Walker, Robinson, Isherwood (B.), Bennett, Isherwood (W.), Moss.
Front: Barber, Fisher, Mycock, Hannah, Wild.

Team Photo 1954/55
(source Brian Isherwood)

Jack Robinson and Brian Isherwood both played for Darwen in the mid 1950s. They were both Darwen lads, which was unusual for the team at the time, and Brian was surprised that the club didn't do more to try and develop talent on a local level.

Brian Isherwood was discovered playing in the Darwen League and joined Darwen in December 1954. He recalls that when he was first selected to play for the team, he was so shy and reserved that, when he arrived at the ground for his first game, rather than tell the gateman that he was in the team, he paid his shilling entrance money to get into the ground.

He was a centre forward and, shortly after scoring 5 goals in a game against Formby, he was selected in January 1955 to play for Lancashire.

Lancashire had been drawn away to Yorkshire in the Northern Counties Amateur Championship and the game was played at Whitby. Alongside Isherwood in the line up was his Darwen team mate Stan Johnston who had become the regular centre half choice for the county, as well as Roy Vernon from Blackburn Rovers.

Despite being the "red rose county", the Lancashire team wore maroon shirts, white shorts and red and white socks and lost to their roses rivals 4-2.

Jack Robinson was in the Darwen youth team that reached the final of the Lancashire Youth Cup in 1951. The game was played at Leyland Motors ground where the Darwen side lost 3-1 to Preston North End. After national service, he returned to play for the senior team for 5 years from 1953 to 1958 before transferring to Netherfield at Kendal.

Bob Eccles recently said of Robinson that the right half *"could head the ball like a rocket. He had more power in his head than David Beckham has in his foot...!"*

Apart from those two seasons at the start of the decade, the Darwen team had little success during the 1950s and 1960s. Brian Isherwood has a few ideas as to the contributing factors.

Player Selections

Unlike the manager/coach arrangement that we know today, the team in those days was selected by a playing committee made up from the board of directors. This was a system that continued well into the 1960s.

Brian remembers that this used to cause a lot of confusion: *"None of them had ever played football. Each would have their favourite players and they would put them forward for any position.."*

"Ken Holliday played right full back for Blackburn Rovers and ended up at Darwen. One of the directors had Ken as his favourite and, if he was outvoted at right back, he'd put him down for left back and right through the team until he got in - it was bit of a nonsense really.... That's no reflection on Ken - he was a nice bloke - that was just the system.."

The hit and miss nature of team selection using this policy is clearly demonstrated in the minutes of a directors' meeting from 9th January 1961 where it was agreed that *"any person who attends the meeting and has attended the previous match be allowed a vote in the selection of the team."*

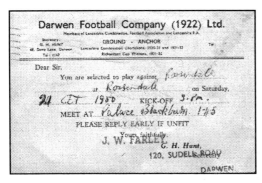

A postal notification of selection from 1950 (source: Edgar Bennett)

111

Tactics

Brian also felt that this "management by committee" meant that the team was never able to play with any tactical awareness:

"They'd say: Right - kick off's at 3 o'clock on Saturday and we'd get there at quarter past or half past two. There'd be no talk, no tactics - we'd all get changed and on we went. When I look back at it now - it was pathetic, really.

I'd been playing football in the army and I knew how they operated then I came to Darwen and I thought there's something wrong here.... We'd have won more matches if we'd have just spent a bit of time talking to each other about what we should be doing and not doing."

However, this was by no means peculiar to Darwen at that time. It was exactly the same with the Lancashire County side which was coached by Rovers' Harry Healless: *" a load of strangers - no talk - there's your shirt there's your shorts get on there and play ..."*

And, of course, there was always the pitch....: *"We had a bad pitch at Darwen. The Darwen end of the pitch was a quagmire - especially with the heavier ball we had then - when you were under the hammer, our defenders couldn't get the ball to the half way line!"*

Off the field, however, Isherwood has nothing but praise for the efforts of the directors: *"They did a good job in keeping the club going despite falling gates and spiralling costs. Local companies did nothing to help. They didn't support the club in the same way as, for example, the cricket club was kept afloat by Crown wallcoverings".*

Sid Brindle

Sid Brindle
(source: Golden Jubilee Book
/ Mrs B Merrick)

An important figure in the Darwen set up at the time was Sid Brindle who had taken over from Joe Bishop as masseur.

Brindle had a private sports physio practice in Victoria Street, Darwen and players with injuries would go to see him at home after Tuesday and Thursday training evenings.

Brian Isherwood has fond memories of Sid Brindle: *"He was just the trainer - the first aid man - and had no input in team selections. He called everybody on the team "pal" They weren't called Brian or Jack or Trevor - he called them all "pal"."*

"Besides having his own practice, he worked at Crown Wallcoverings where he was the first aider and he had a lot of facilities. I used to slip out of work and pop over to Crown for a bit of treatment, which was convenient."

Bob Eccles recalls: *"if he told a player they were not to play on the following Saturday and they did so without his permission, he would wash his hands of them"*.

Professionals and Amateurs

In those days, the Lancashire Combination and the Cheshire County League represented the same level of football that the Conference and the Northern Premier League do today. As such clubs like Darwen, Nelson et al used to be able to have one or two ex league players in the team to help train up the youngsters and the presence of those players would add a few extra onto the attendance.

Les Pilkington was one such player. The inside right had originally come from Darwen and then played for Arsenal and Watford before returning to Darwen at the end of his career. One day before a game, a spectator asked the gateman if Les Pilkington was playing. Upon being told no, the man turned on his heels and left. Having been over heard, the gateman was instructed in no uncertain terms not to tell people that sort of thing in future until they had paid to come in...!

Brian Isherwood also rated Pilkington: *"Les Pilkington was an intelligent player. He stands out more in my eyes from the team at the time. Slightly selfish, but that's academic. There were a lot of times when he could have slipped it through - but he didn't."*

Other ex pros that Bob Eccles recalls having played for Darwen include Ernie Robey of Bolton, Roy Hatsall of Preston North End and Roy Fawcett who was understudy to Stanley Matthews at Blackpool. There was also Charlie Cowsill (ex Bolton): *"a very useful utility player but a very poor trainer, and often missed sessions. He was still the fittest player on the team as he was a window cleaner and was up and down ladders all day long"*.

Other players that Jack Robinson remembers from the 1950s include: Jack Chew and Reg Attwell both formerly of Burnley and Willy Kelly, Jack Patterson, Tommy McManus and Frank Chadwick of Blackburn Rovers

Along with the ex league players, teams of Darwen's calibre also attracted many "nearly men" - such as Bill Isherwood (no relation to Brian) and Norman Smith who both had spells with Arsenal reserves without really managing to break through to the first team.

Stan Johnston, team captain, on the other hand, was a pure amateur and only got paid travel expenses whereas some of the others got paid as part time professionals. The ex league players got the most money because of their experience and reputations but, according to Robinson, it was not always deserved: *"Jackie Chew was great - he'd take time afterwards to sit down and talk about the game but many of the others were only interested in the money."*

Brian Isherwood goes along with this view: *"The pros had dropped out of the league. They were getting on a bit and it was probably easy money for them at that time. In the league they got about £12 per week but there's no way that Darwen could offer that. The top players probably wouldn't have got more than a fiver a week - that's just a guess. All I got was what they called "expenses" - about 7/6."*

But, despite the varying levels of experience and ability within the team, *"there was never any bickering even when we got stuffed. There was never any going off and giving someone what for if they made a mistake - but we were like 11 relative strangers."*

Jack Robinson recalls the joys of travelling away to evening games in far off locations such as New Brighton, Kendal or Barrow in the days before the motorways were built: *"You'd have to leave work early if it was a midweek match. The coach would pick people up at different spots on the way and drop them off on the way back - we often wouldn't get back home until twelve o'clock at night"*

Bob Eccles agrees: *"FA Cup replays used to have to be played on or before the following Thursday so they had to be played on weekday afternoons, requiring a 2.15 kick off to miss the dark evenings. The team would often have to leave Darwen early to get to the venue".*

Playing away at Netherfield (Kendal) was one of the longest trips in the 1960s. While nowadays it is only a 1 hour drive, in those days the team had to leave Darwen at 10.30 am for a 3pm kick-off. The coach would stop off at Carnforth for lunch and the players would have a special meal of egg on toast and rice pudding (and nothing else…). Upon arrival, the players would have to walk the last ½ mile up to the ground to exercise after their long journey.

Trying to get time off work was a big problem for players in those days and that was what brought an end to Brian Ishwerwood's Darwen career.

In the days when Saturday mornings were part of the normal working week, he would often have to ask for an hour off - especially if there was an away game. He had turned down the chance of playing professionally (both Southport and Grimsby had made him an offer); *"I was keen on football but not so keen as to make it my living. I'd rather have stayed in the papertrade."*

"But then I came unstuck as it was causing trouble with other members of the staff. It got to the point where the bosses said: look - what are you going to do: are you going to be a footballer or are you going to work in a paper mill? So I had to give up playing altogether and concentrate on work."

1950/51 matchday
programme
(source: Edgar Bennett)

116

Floodlights in the 50s.

Jack Robinson recalls the days before floodlights: *"One particular thing I remember - we used to go training at nights in winter time and we used to have a lamp at each corner of the ground - like oil tilly lamps. Training was always a bit of gamble. It was so dark at the Anchor with just those lamps in the corner"*

Training was also dangerous for another reason - the groundsman Jim Martin was very protective of his playing surface and didn't like anyone going onto it in case they cut it up.

Of the advent of floodlights Jack said: *"Accrington Stanley was one of the first teams in the area to have floodlights and they were stuck on top of telegraph poles! They weren't the best in the world. When the ball went up in the air you'd lose track of it - then it would suddenly appear!"*

To celebrate having their floodlights, Accrington Stanley organised a floodlit competition between the local clubs - Darwen, Nelson Padiham etc which Darwen won - one of the few accolades that they would win in an otherwise barren period.

Weekly Business

A Minute Book for the directors meetings for the period March 1959 to May 1961 recently came to light and certain items which, at the time, may have been quite run of the mill in their own context, are worthy of note some 40 years on:

6th April 1959: *"roller at the Walpamur Green. This was ours but had been given by our late chairman with a promise of free paint as long as we require same"*.

20th April 1959: *"the inspector of police had asked for two tickets for the Cup Final - this was refused"*.

117

6th July 1959: *Price of admission to be raised to 1/3. Season tickets - yellow complimentary, Blue 50 at 25/-, Pink 100 at 12/6.*

21st September 1959: *J Howarth took over as secretary following the resignation of J Farley*

21st September 1959: *decided to write to Blackburn Rover re electric account stating that the directors of Darwen FC felt that some of the liability is theirs as ground expenses*

12th October 1959: *"that Ronnie Orr be given two weeks away to train at Burnden Park until he gets his autocycle repaired"*

16th May 1960: *"any player who did not do any training during the coming season would be suspended"*

8th August 1960: *"that the Ladies Committee may attend the meeting but that if they wish to vote at a meeting they must sign with the rest of the committee for a bank overdraft"*

17th October 1960: *"that the telephone be left on the ground and secretary write to telephone manager re account received".*

19th December 1960: *"that bonus be increased for the remainder of the season to 12/- for a win to players in team only plus 12th man".*

The 1960s

As Darwen Football Club edged towards a new decade, it was clear that the club was, once again, heading for serious financial trouble.

At a directors' meeting on 24th March 1959, it was minuted that *"it was a shame that a town with a population of over 30.000 we could only get about 300 to the Anchor"* and, in October, Chairman R Jepson said: *"with the present gate receipts it is impossible to carry on a successful team"*

By then it was impossible to attract new investment into the club from outside. S Howarth reported that: *"the directors were below strength but people had been asked to serve on the board but no-one was willing"* and by the end of the 1959/60 season, the club was in such a state that it couldn't afford to pay outstanding wages to the players: *"each player who was owed wages at the end of the season be sent £2 each on account"*.

On 16th June 1960 an open meeting was held at the Provident Hall in Darwen to try and save the club from going bust.

The result was a "Save Our Soccer" committee which was formed to take over the football club and ensure its future. The new committee was set up by the Darwen Supporters Club which had offices in Foundry Street at that time.

It was resolved that the limited company which had been in place since 1922 to run the club be dissolved and reformed as a Football Club as the operating regulations would be less stringent and it would be easier to appoint new directors.

The new committee met 4 days later at the Foundry Street office to set to work. Bill Holden was elected as chairman, Jack Howarth as Honorary Secretary and a very young Bob Eccles found himself in the role of treasurer. Separate sub committees were also set up to oversee specialised areas such as finance, playing staff and ground facilities.

Bob Eccles worked tirelessly for Darwen Football club for some 20 years. He was chairman of the club in the 1970s and is now a Vice President of the North West Counties Football League. However, he recalls that it was not easy going at the start and recounts a story from around that time:

"I used to take the train to Bolton and have my driving lessons there so no-one would know and then I passed his test. I'd been saving up to buy my first car - a Vauxhall Viva at £564. The club had problems with money - It was a do or die situation. Bill Holden was chairman at the time.

One Thursday evening under the Darwen End stand - it was October/November and we had got beaten in the FA Cup. When you lost in the FA Cup in those days it was criminal because that's where the money was - because we used to get quite good crowds in the FA Cup against Morecambe and so on such like.

I said to him "Bill - we can't pay out on Saturday without going to the bank for an overdraft." He said to me: "What we'll do - thee and me - we'll put £500 apiece in - it'll see thee right to the end o't season".

How he knew I had £500 as an 18 year old, I do not know. So we did it and bang went my new car. I had to start saving up all over again and ended up having to wait until 1964 for my car !!!"

Not surprisingly, considering the precarious state of the club during the early 60s, Darwen were relegated from Division One of the Combination at the end of the 1962/63 season.

They spent four years in the Second Division punctuated only by one promotion season in which they finished 3rd. This gave them promotion to the First Division only to drop straight back down again after just one season.

In 1966, the board made the shrewd appointment of Paddy Sowden as team manager. He had played professionally with Blackpool and

Accrington Stanley and had been given a 5 year contract by Darwen with the aim rebuilding the team.

Sowden set his stall out right away and immediately swooped for top Combination goalkeeper Lindsay Wallace, who was then at Clitheroe: *"I was one of his first signings. I'd always been a friend of Paddy's and knew him very well. I'd played against him when he played for Chorley and he was a good coach."*

Sowden's new team blended young Darweners with experienced semi-pros and they won promotion from the Second Division at the first attempt, finishing second in the table to Oldham Reserves.

The arrival of an ex pro as team manager brought a new sense of professionalism to the club. Under Paddy Sowden, the club even introduced smart neck ties for the players and, at that time they were the only club in the Combination to have them. The tie was designed by Sowden himself, showing Darwen tower. If a player or club official turned up without his tie they were fined ½ crown!

Of players from that period, Lindsay Wallace gives particular mention to: *"Ken Garrighty - he was skipper at time ex Accrington Stanley and Chorley - a good classic player. Sean Gallagher - ex Lancaster player - a good winger. Roy Fawcett - he had been understudy to Stanley Matthews at Blackpool and Peter Ashton - a good player - very quick.*

"Paddy also threw in a couple of lads in that came from University - a lad called Ced Gelling, then there was Clender and Faulkener".

Bob Eccles also remembers Peter Ashton: *"A prolific scorer. He had what I call had lucky feet. He wasn't a footballer but when he had the ball to his feet in the penalty area - it was a goal."*

Also worthy of mention from that time are the three Waddicor brothers, Gordon, Les and Michael. Eccles recalls Les Waddicor (left winger) as *"the only player I have ever seen score a hat-trick direct from corners".*

Darwen were promoted back to the Division 1 again at the end of the 1967/68 season but struggled to finish anywhere higher than mid table for the next 4 seasons.

By then Paddy Sowden had moved on. As is often the case, his success in his first year at Darwen put him in the limelight and he was quickly snatched up by Horwich RMI. From there he became youth team manager at Blackpool and then commercial manager at Luton Town.

Jimmy Harkness had been playing the team and took over as manager but the impetus was lost.

Darwen FC Share Certificate
(Source: Bob Eccles)

The 1970s

Even in the early 60s Darwen had been getting reasonably good crowds. Many people remember how flects of buses used to go from the town centre to the Anchor Ground and there were even buses from Ewood Park to the Anchor as well. At the end of a match there would often be 8 or 9 buses waiting at the top of the Anchor Estate to take the spectators back to town.

During the course of the 1960s, however, support for Lancashire Combination football had dwindled as many of the top clubs moved on to the Northern Premier League and the Cheshire County League.

The situation got so bad that in 1968, the Second Division was scrapped all together and all remaining clubs were merged into a single division Lancashire Combination.

To compensate for the reduction in attractive fixtures during this period, the Combination committee, quite possibly learning from the experience of the Lancs FA back in the 1880s, introduced two new knockout tournaments - the George Watson Challenge Trophy in 1969/70 and the Bridge Shield in 1970/71.

By the 1971/72 season, things once again looked bad for Darwen Football Club. The brief optimism of the Paddy Sowden era was long gone and it was only due to a fortunate run of 5 wins from 6 games at the end of the season pulled them sufficiently high up the table that they avoided having to apply for re-election. With many new teams looking to step up to the Combination at that time, it was not a foregone conclusion that they would have been voted back in.

The club was, once again, strapped for cash and they had to relinquish the services of both coach and groundsman to cut costs.

Then, one cold windy night in February, something happened that would change the Darwen club for the better. Stewart Johnson had been a player at Darwen before going to play in the Bury district.

Glyn Watson was manager of a team in the Manchester Amateur League called Clarence Athletic and the pair of them turned up at the Anchor Ground one night out of the blue and asked whether the Clarence club could merge with Darwen.

Bob Eccles who was, by then, chairman of the flagging club weighed up the pros and cons: *"Darwen was not in the best of health either financially or player wise. whereus Clarence had a good side at the time. After a bit of give and take, Darwen agreed to wear their colours of claret and blue."*

Bob Eccles
(source Jack Howarth)

Thus it was agreed to merge the two clubs and their playing staff, although the club would still be called Darwen Football Club.

The existing Darwen players were given the option of staying but many chose to leave and went to play for other clubs and, as Darwen's manager Jimmy Harkness had already left, Glyn Watson took over at the helm of the new combined team. Once the merger had been agreed between Darwen FC and Clarence Athletic, the Clarence players gradually began playing for Darwen.

As Jack Haworth, serving club secretary at the time, recalls: *"they'd play for Clarence on Saturday afternoons and if they didn't have a night match and Darwen did, they'd come along and play for Darwen midweek."*

The move certainly enabled Darwen to guarantee their place in the Combination and would, over the next 3 years, bring Darwen Football Club its best days since the 1930s. Bob Eccles agrees: *"Their players merged with ours and became the team that won the league and the cups. Without them coming in, we would not have been as successful as we were."*

1972/73 League Campaign

For the new season, Darwen FC broke with over 50 years of tradition and took to the field wearing Clarence's sky blue and claret instead of their traditional red but any disgruntled fans will have soon warmed to the new arrangement once play got underway.

In the first game of the season they were at home to the Accrington Stanley side that had finished runners up the year before and started the campaign off with a morale boosting 1-1 draw, courtesy of a Frank O'Kane goal.

O'Kane had been one of the players to arrive from Clarence and was quick to make an impression on the Darwen public as he found the net in each of his first 4 games and hit a hat-trick in the 4-2 win over Wigan Rovers on 5th September.

Hopkinson also proved to be a hotshot in front of goal, as he notched up 10 goals in the first 11 games

In the period up to Christmas 1972, Darwen lost only one league game - 1-0 away at Ford Motors in September. Following that they embarked on a 15 match unbeaten run, winning 13 games and drawing just 2, which didn't see them lose again in the league until a 2-3 defeat at Accrington on 3rd February.

But that was merely a blip and Darwen only lost two more games all season - 0-2 away at Ashton Town and 2-3 at Blackpool Mechanics.

Following that defeat at Blackpool on 14th April, they won each of their last 5 games, scoring 19 goals and conceding just 2.

The title winning game came away at St Helens on 28th April where a 1-0 victory, courtesy of Frank O'Kane's 30th league and cup goal of the season, ensured that Darwen could not be caught by fellow contenders Bacup and Accrington

Darwen Advertiser & News – 3.5.73
(source: Bob Eccles)

The trophy was presented to Darwen captain Tony Burke by the Mayor of Darwen Cllr. Philip Clear in front of 500 fans at the Anchor Ground following a 3-1 win over Blackpool Mechanics on Tuesday 1st May.

Chairman Eccles said: *"from the start of the season we have always tried to play attacking and entertaining football and it has paid handsome dividends".*

Winning the title mean that Darwen could now apply to the Northern Premier League - the highest level of non league football at that time - but Eccles did not feel the time was right: *"I don't think we are ready for it from both a playing and financial point of view".*

Lindsay Wallace: Record Breaker

In a career spanning 20 years Darwen goalkeeper Lindsay Wallace appeared in a record 784 Combination league and cup games.

He started off with Preston North End's "A" team as an 18 year old but, after suffering an injury at the age of 20, joined Clitheroe in the Lancashire Combination. After 15 years at Clitheroe, during which he broke the club record for appearances, he found himself looking for a new challenge and was encouraged to sign for Darwen by Paddy Sowden, who was rebuilding the team that had been relegated to the second division.

Wallace moved to Darwen for the 1967/68 season and the newly constructed team won promotion back to the Lancashire combination first division at the first time of asking. During his time at Darwen, Wallace broke the previous Combination record of 750 appearances - held by Johnny Clarke for Rossendale - and was part of the team that won the Combination championship in 1973.

Upon his retirement at the end of the 1972/73 season, a testimonial game was held for him at the Anchor Ground . Unfortunately, heavy rain had a disastrous effect on the turnout but the few hundred who braved the weather saw a good game between a Lindsay Wallace XI and an All Stars XI. Players who took part included:

- Liverpool legend and 1966 World Cup winner Roger Hunt,
- Former Blackburn Rovers skipper and 35 times England international Ronnie Clayton
- Bryan Douglas - Blackburn Rovers (509 games 117 goals) and England (36 caps)
- Adam Blacklaw - ex Scotland, Burnley and Blackburn goalkeeper
- John Connely 20 caps for England. League championship medals with Burnley and Man Utd.
- Ray Parry - FA Cup winner with Bolton wanderers
- Brian Pilkington - former Burnley and England winger

- Mick McGrath - former Blackburn Rovers and Republic of Ireland wing half
- John Byrom and Warwick Hughes - members of Bolton Wanderers 1973 third division winning side.

To commemorate his achievement, Blackburn artist Norman Hughes presented Lindsay Wallace with a special tableau bearing the Darwen and Clitheroe colours. Inside is an inscription which says:

"This tableau records that on May 9th 1973 at the Anchor Ground Darwen a testimonial match was staged to mark the retirement from soccer of Lindsay Wallace after a period in the Lancs Combination with Clitheroe FC and Darwen FC extending over 20 years during which time he made the record breaking total of 784 appearances this tribute not only denotes this feat but Lindsay's super sportsmanship which reflects the highest distinction brought to the game."

1973/74 Season

Keen to repeat their Championship win, many people at Darwen may have found the 1973/74 season a bit of a disappointment after they could "only" manage second place in the Combination.

Accrington Stanley took the title, finishing 5 points ahead of Darwen and Bacup who were level on 58 points each.

Frank O'Kane
(source: A Holden)

However, Darwen's Frank O'Kane's 50th minute equaliser in the super 1-1 away draw at Accrington in the final game of the season on 11th May was all important as it ensured not only a valuable point but also that Darwen would finish with a superior goal average by less than one goal over Bacup!

1974 Bass Charington Cup Final

Darwen were also to finish second best in the Cup Final - played at Burscough's Victoria Park on Wednesday 15th May - where they were matched against St Helens Town who had finished 5th in the Combination 8 points behind Darwen and Bacup

Darwen found themselves 2-0 down by half time but came out for the second half all fired up and determining to give a better account of themselves.

The half time team talk must have worked as Barry Lord pulled a goal back within a minute. But this joy was short lived as, from the resulting kick off, St Helens centre forward Merrill raced straight up to the other end of the field and scored again to make it 1-3.

Lord struck again on 55 minutes to peg the deficit back to a single goal but 8 minutes later a fortuitous penalty enabled St Helens to restore their 2 goal cushion. But Darwen were still not out of the running and team captain Tony Burke headed home a left wing corner to score the fifth goal in a frenetic 20 minute period, bringing the score to 3-4.

Both sides had more chances to add to the tally but all too soon, the referee blew his whistle and brought to an end a final which Lancashire Combination president Wesley Bridge afterwards described as "fantastic".

1974/75 League Campaign

In the two previous seasons under Glyn Watson as manager, Darwen had won the title in 1972/73 and finished runners up to local rivals Accrington Stanley in 1973/74.

With six of the side that had played in the 1973 championship team still in place - Steve Collins, Barry Haymer, Steve Waywell, Barry Lord, Frank O'Kane and Keith Richards - going into the new season, Darwen were definitely one of the favourites to become Lancashire Combination champions again in 1974/75

They started off in explosive fashion, beating Prescot Town 5-0 at the anchor ground in the first game of the new season with Frank O'Kane scoring a hat-trick.

It was almost a case of "déjà-vu" as the Anchormen put together another impressive string of results similar to the one that had landed them the 1973 title. After a couple of away defeats early in the season - at Leyland Motors (0-1) and Wren Rovers (0-2) - they went unbeaten for 12 games and the 3-4 defeat away at Kirkby Town on 8th February was the last game that they lost all season.

This time around, the goals were more evenly spread than before with players like Alan Hiley and Barry Lord getting on the scoresheet regularly while Keith Richards had a quieter start to the season and did not really get into his stride until well into April.

It turned out to be one of the closest finishing title races ever with just one point separating the "Darreners" from second placed Blackpool Mechanics. This would turn out to be the tightest winning margin for 7 years and Darwen's 0-0 draw away at Blackpool in March was a crucial result in deciding the destiny of the title.

They were left just needing a single point from the last game - ironically at home to Blackpool Mechanics.

Unfortunately the club was told before the game by the Lancashire Combination committee that, even if they got the point they needed, they would not be presented with the trophy after the match and would have to wait until the Combination Cup game against Bootle the following Wednesday.

Chairman Bob Eccles put the decision down to sour grapes: *"I have the feeling they are not cooperating with us because we are determined to join the Cheshire League"*.

The midweek cup clash with Bootle would clash with Blackburn Rovers - who were going to be presented with the Third Division trophy before a friendly match with Coventry City - and would, therefore, deprive near neighbours Darwen of a potential bumper crowd. The Combination also refused permission for the cup game to be switched to the Tuesday evening instead.

Prior to the all important Blackpool game on Sunday 4th May, Darwen were handed more bad news with the announcement that top scorer Frank O'Kane, with 30 goals to his credit so far from the campaign, might be missing with a groin strain.

As things turned out, Eccles was proved right. Darwen's biggest crowd for 15 years - over 1600 fans - crowded into the Anchor Ground to watch the title decider, many of them new faces wearing

Blackburn scarves who had come to see the special occasion and most of whom would be at Ewood Park come Wednesday.

Ronnie Haworth gave Darwen the lead after just 4 minutes but Blackpool needed to win both this game and their last one against Nelson so they fought back hard. The pressure paid off. They equalised in the 58th minute and then took lead 6 minutes later.

Just as it looked as if the title was slipping away from Darwen's grasp, they were awarded a disputed penalty for handball 8 minutes from time. Martin Farnworth - the youngest player on the field - coolly slotted the ball away to clinch the draw and the title.

Combination Cup Final

Keith Richards
(source: Jack Haworth)

The first leg of the Combination Cup final was held at the Anchor ground and Darwen swept into an early lead with a Frank O'Kane goal in the 20th minute.

Keith Richards scored a second just before halftime and the same player scored a third midway through the second half as he headed in a Martin Farnworth cross.

Tensions boiled over in the last 15 minutes and Bootle's Mortimer was booked for an incident on Richards. After the final whistle had gone, Richards was again the target and was knocked to the ground in a scuffle as the teams left the field.

In the second leg, 3 days later, Darwen's comfortable three-goal advantage into took a knock as early as the second minute when ex Everton player John O'Leary gave the Merseysiders an early breakthrough.

Bob Barras headed a Darwen equaliser from a Tony Burke free kick to ensure the teams left the field level pegging at half time and Darwen's three goal lead overall remained battered but intact.

However, with goalkeeper Dave Collins limping from a first half injury, Darwen were hit for two goals in the space of 4 minutes on the hour mark as Bootle fired themselves back into contention.

The Darwen net then came under siege as the home side tried to make the most of home advantage. But, as Darwen nerves began to fray, Keith Richards gratefully swooped in on a Martin Farnworth cross to give the reds a two goal cushion.

Bootle won 3-2 on the night but Darwen's first leg goals were the deciding factor. The final aggregate score of 5-3 gave them the Combination league cup and prestigious league and cup double.

Darwen FC - 1975 League & Cup Winners
Back: G Watson, Howard, ?, Barras, Collins, Lord, Richards, Waywell, Taylor, B Waters
Front: Lock, Burke, Meadowcroft, Howarth, O'Kane, Hamer, Hiley, ?, McGinley
(source Darwen FC)

Cheshire League Application

With the league championship still very much undecided and three big games still to go, Darwen had already boldly announced after their 4-2 win over St Helens on Easter Monday that they intended to leave the Lancashire Combination after 80 years and apply to join the Cheshire County League instead.

Several of the top teams had left the Combination in recent years and, as such, the standard had slipped. Club Chairman Bob Eccles explained that the move would mean a better standard of football and better support from visiting clubs.

The club had first attempted such a move back in the 1930s but this time around, the signs were good. Two clubs were going to resign from the Cheshire League and Darwen were hoping to land one of the vacant places.

The move was not greeted by everyone, however. Accrington Stanley's chairman Bill Parkinson said that " *Lancashire clubs should not be allowed to play in the Cheshire League*" and called upon those clubs that had switched in recent years to come back and replace the Liverpool clubs who should, more rightly, be playing in the Cheshire League.

On the same day as Darwen's league cup final win away at Bootle, the Cheshire League's annual meeting on 9th May voted unanimously to allow them to join for the 1975/76 season, along with fellow Combination team St Helens. Bob Eccles was Darwen chairman at the time of the move into the Cheshire League. Speaking some 25 years afterwards, he still feels the move was justified at the time: *"We'd won everything. The Lancashire Combination wasn't strong enough for us then. We just wanted to better ourselves again."*

Looking at the statistics, there could be little doubt of that assertion. In the 3 seasons since the merger with Clarence Athletic, Darwen achieved 2 league championships, 1 league runners up place, 1 league cup, 1 cup runners up and one semi final place.

Under Glyn Watson they suffered just 12 league defeats in 3 seasons with only one coming at home but once up in the Cheshire League, Darwen FC immediately found life much more difficult. The club hadn't got the resources or the people to bring the money in like the other bigger clubs could.

There were some big teams in the Cheshire League including Chorley, Hyde and Leek who are now in the Northern Premier League, Horwich who are now in the Conference and, of course, Wigan Athletic who were successfully voted into the Football League. Darwen was now a very small fish in a very big pond.

They found it harder to compete and so, as Jack Howarth recalls, one by one, the top players were poached by clubs who came in offering better wages. Prolific goalscorer Frank O'Kane was one of the first of the big names to leave, being lured away by high spending Droylsden.

This, in turn, had a negative effect on attendances. The team didn't win as many games in the Cheshire League as they had in the Combination. Bob Eccles explains: *"People are fickle - they'll only follow a winning team. But it's no good winning 10 games on the trot and expecting gates to treble. You have to win trophies before people start taking notice."*

Things got to the point where a change was needed - Glyn Watson was sacked. Bob Eccles said: *"We'd had a bad run and the committee decided it needed a change. We said that, if we didn't win the next game at Nelson, we'd have to ask him to resign, I asked him, he declined so I sacked him.*

"Glyn had worked very hard for the club and it's only when you're down that you're kicked out. He'd brought a team into Darwen that was very successful. He worked very hard for the club - his mother washed the kit. It was sad that he had to go - but that's football. You get bigger people than Glyn and myself who get hatched and despatched for very small reasons."

Jimmy Birkett

The man who came in to succeed Glyn Watson as manager and take on the task of shoring up the crumbling side was Jimmy Birkett.

He had started off as a player with Accrington Stanley before the *"Gilbraith Scottish era"* playing for a 1½ seasons in their "A"team. He played one central league game for Blackburn Rovers and then moved on to Southport reserves

Jimmy Birkett
(source: Jack Haworth)

Once in non league, he had - in his own words *"more clubs than Tony Jacklin"*, playing semi pro at Nelson, Netherfield, Rossendale, Chorley, Darwen, Clitheroe and Great Harwood

Birkett only played for Darwen for half a season in 1960/61. The team at the time included Matt Busby's son and Jackie Patterson - ex Blackburn Rovers -in goal.

Managerial Appointment

Birkett had moved into coaching at Great Harwood in the Northern Premier League and later moved on to Clitheroe. While on an FA coaching course as Lilleshall, he met Jack Prytherch who had been assistant manager at Darwen under Glyn Watson.

"Playing in the Cheshire League, they struggled. Glyn went and Jack Pytherch knew me through this coaching course. He didn't want to be manager, although it was his job if he'd wanted it - he was a top class man"

"He asked if I'd be interested in taking the Darwen job. I thought about it - Darwen was step up from Clitheroe - so I went for an interview and got the job".

Of course, by the time that Birkett arrived at Darwen, things were in a bit of a mess: *"When Glyn went, the wage bill dropped and we lost half the players. When he packed up all the training facilities were in Bolton. We used to travel to Bolton and we were never sure if the park was going to be open or not. When we got there sometimes it was shut and we just trained in the streets."*

"My asset was that I was a motivator. Management was the hardest job I ever had but I loved coaching and I loved training. "In my day training had been a boring session so I always tried to make it interesting"

Notable players who Jimmy recalls from his days as Darwen manager include:

- Fred Roberts; *"top class goalkeeper - on a par with Lindsay Wallace."*
- Ronnie Brooks: *"captain - he was the rock of the defence - the team was built round him".*
- Gary Johnson: *" had been a pro footballer - just lacked a bit of pace"*
- Dick Grogan: *"good player - he played NPL football with Harwood I got him at the end of his career"*

Good and Bad Transfer Deals

Bob Eccles recalls that his first sale as chairman was when Derek Lever transferred to Wigan Athletic along with goalkeeper Edgar Bennett for £100.

His record sale as chairman of Darwen was Steve Mullen who signed for Bury in 1978. Eddie Quigley - Bury manager at the time - enquired about the player and when he offered £3.000 for him, Eccles could not get the deal done quickly enough, such was the club's financial plight at that time, in his own words: *"I snatched his hand off..."*

Jimmy Birkett also speaks highly of Steve Mullen, describing him as his *"finest acquisition":*

"He was playing in the Darwen League v Clitheroe League match. I spotted this lad, a bit chunky, not too tall but what an ability! I was frightened to death and was looking around to see if anyone else was watching him. As soon as the game finished I went and got his signature.

Steve Mullen
(source: Jack Haworth)

That lad should have been a professional footballer. No doubt about it. Man City were looking at him to sign him but he had a falling out with Bury at the end of the season over money and walked out of the club and came back to Darwen. It was great for us but I was devastated ..! The best player I ever handled - he was class."

One bad piece of business that Bob Eccles recalls involved local lad John Waddington. Bill Shankly had called up to say that Liverpool wanted to take a look at the player and asked if they could play him in a reserves game at Bolton.

Bob Eccles gave permission for Waddington to play and, after the game, Shankly said that he was interested in him and not to let anyone else have him. The player was signed for Darwen as an amateur and therefore could not command a fee between the clubs, and, trusting Shankly, Eccles resisted the temptation to sign Waddington on a semi pro basis and thus increase his value.

Liverpool signed Waddington and said they would give Darwen an ex-gratia payment which, although the player was certainly worth several thousand, only amounted to £50. Eccles felt very let down by Shankly, calling the figure *"an insult"* and vowed never to offer another promising player to Liverpool again.

Fund Raising

Having moved into a bigger league and requiring greater expendtiure, Darwen Football Club found itself losing money.

Bob Eccles organised the club's first sportsman's dinner to try and boost the dwindling funds with the help of his good friend, Peter Swailes, Manchester City chairman at the time, and Derek Keighley, later Blackburn Rovers chairman, who both spoke at the dinner:
"It was things that like that kept the club going financially - Like the Manchester City friendly game. Peter Swailes brought the team as a favour to me. They played a strong side that included Bryan Kidd."

Friendly game v Manchester City

The game in question was a warm up match for the 1979/80 Cheshire League season and Darwen played host to Manchester City at the Anchor Ground. The game attracted a good sized crowd - despite unpleasant weather conditions - and ended up with a 2-1 win for the prestigious visitors. George Isherwood was the Darwen scorer.

Jimmy Birkett recalls: *"Bryan Kidd played that day nd impressed me as to what a nice bloke he was. Some of the others were terrible.*

"Steve Mullen was playing for Darwen and he was too good for one or two of the City players. So one of their England players kept giving him a bit of stick. Geoff Robinson was a big lad - a scouser - and went over to this bloke and said if you touch him again I'll give you two black eyes. The other chap was a renowned hard man in the Football League but he kept quite after that!!!".

In August 1979 a new bombshell landed on Darwen when Bob Eccles was deposed as chairman by his fellow directors. He refused the offer to stay on the board as a director and had no further involvement with Darwen Football Club, although he has remained in touch with north west football as a league official.

Another Setback - Arson Attack

In the 4 seasons that Jimmy Birkett had been in charge at Darwen he had managed to slowly turn the team around from being a bottom of the table side (they finished 19th out of 22 then 15th out of 22 in his first two seasons) into a top 10 side with a 10th place finish in season 1979/80.

But, just as it was beginning to look as if the club had turned the corner, another disaster struck. The old main stand had been falling down bit by bit for many years and, by 1980, was a far cry from the magnificent structure that it had been in the club's heyday of the 1930s.

In June of that year, vandals achieved in one night what the elements had not managed to do in 40 years, as Darwen Football Club fell victim to a mystery blaze which destroyed what had remained of the stand and the changing rooms that were housed beneath it. Donations were urgently sought to help with the rebuilding costs - thought to be around £15.000 - and the Cheshire League showed their support by allowing the team to play their first 9 league games of the new season away from home.

Birkett recalls: *"That was the worst time I ever spent as manager because we lost a lot of support and, when we got home, we couldn't win a match for love nor nowt"*

The team managed to scrape together a few draws from their opening games but it is hard enough to play away at the best of times, without having to play away all the time.

Eventually a Portakabin was installed at the Anchor Ground to act as changing rooms but, by the time they were able to play at home again, the team's confidence was shattered.

Chapter Five
North West Counties

Background

The age-old problem of Lancashire clubs choosing to join the Cheshire County League was finally resolved in 1982, when the two leagues amalgamated to form the North West Counties Football League.

The idea was to formalise the next tier down of the non-league football pyramid and, as such, the new league would, along with the Northern Counties (East) League and the Northern League, act as a feeder to the Northern Premier League. In turn, the NWCFL has formal promotion/relegation arrangements with the Liverpool County Combination, the Manchester League, the Mid-Cheshire League, the Midland League, the West Cheshire League and the West Lancashire League.

The new league initially had three divisions with promotion and relegation - subject to ground grading requirements - however, it was reduced to two divisions at the end of the 1986-87 season, due to the formation of a First Division of the Northern Premier League – currently known as the *Unibond League*.

After struggling for the whole of their time in the Cheshire County League, Darwen managed a top 10 finish for the one and only time in the 1981/82, coming 6th and that final placing gave them a place in Division One for the first season of the NWCFL.

NWCFL Challenge Cup

In their first season in the new amalgamated league, Darwen carried on where they had left off in the Cheshire League and finished a very creditable 6th in the First Division.

They crowned a successful season by reaching the first ever NWCFL Challenge Cup final. They beat Warrington 3-0 at the Anchor Ground in the semi final, with goals from Grant Lightbown (2), and Paul Goldsbrough, to set up a final with Skelmersdale of the Second Division.

Although the Darreners were favourites to win the final, manager Jimmy Birkett called for caution: *"We shall certainly not make the mistake of being over confident simply because there is a division between the teams."*

Darwen FC - 1983 NWCFL Cup Final
Darling, Birkett, Higgins, Jones, Roberts, Smith, Jones, Brooks, Martin
Ainscough, Goldsbrough, Benko, Lightbown, Whittaker
(Source: Jimmy Birkett)

142

The final was played at Bury's Gigg Lane ground on 5th May and did not go entirely as planned. After a dreary goalless first half, the game came to life in the 57th minute when Skelmersdale took a shock lead with a shot that ricocheted in off the goalpost.

Paul Goldsbrough equalised for Darwen two minutes later when a Ronnie Brooks header came back off the bar and the match remained very much in the balance for the last 30 minutes.

Extra time followed and Skelmersdale substitute Paul Gannon scored with his very first touch of the game with just 10 minutes left to play. Seconds ticked away and Darwen piled on the pressure. John Ainscough sent a cross high into the goal mouth and, in the resulting scramble, Ian Whittaker fired the ball into the net for a last gasp equaliser.

In a recent interview, Birkett recalled how lucky Darwen had been: *"We snatched it out of the fire at Bury. They had already put the Skelmersdale tapes on the cup and Darwen equalised in the very last minute."*

Darwen won the toss for the venue for the replay but as they had home advantage, it meant that, if it was a draw at the end of the game, Skelmersdale would win the cup on away goals.

The replay took place at the Anchor Ground on Tuesday 10th May. 700 fans braved the pouring rain and the pitch looked more like a ploughed field than a sports ground.

Despite having home advantage, Darwen made it look very hard work. As Birkett recalls: *"Skelmersdale played out of their socks"* and took the lead after 57 minutes but, six minutes later, Mick Higgins beat the "Skem" offside trap and ran on to a John Ainscough pass to level the score with a superb solo effort.

Once again, the score remained level at full time and 30 minutes extra time was played. During this period, the visitors resorted to all sorts of delaying tactics as the minutes ticked away, knowing that a draw would hand them the cup.

Once again, it looked as if Skelmersdale ribbons would be on the trophy but Darwen's late late show did it again. With two minutes remaining, Grant Lightbown burst down the left hand side, beat two defenders and crossed. His striking partner Paul Goldsbrough met the cross and slotted the ball away from close range.

The Anchor Ground erupted as Darwen celebrated their first major trophy win since 1975.

After the game Jimmy Birkett was deservedly happy: *"It's been the biggest night in my time at Darwen and it's the perfect way to step down as team manager."*

Club Chairman Dennis Jepson said: *"I am absolutely delighted for both the team and for Jimmy. The support we received on a dreadful night was tremendous and the players kept going to the end."*

1983 Cup Winners!
Jimmy Birkett and the Darwen players with the cup
<small>(Source: Lancashire Evening Telegraph)</small>

Mick Higgins was one of the players who played in the successful cup winning team.

He had started off playing in the league with Blackburn Rovers and Workington, before an achilles injury meant he had to drop into non league. After spells with Rossendale, Stalybridge, Chorley and Accrington, he was enticed to Darwen by Jimmy Birkett for the 1982/83 season.

He was attracted to Darwen as he already knew several of the players and was impressed with the side that Birkett had built up: *"It was a good solid side: Fred Roberts in goal - there was Ronnie Brooks the captain – he took no prisoners, Steve Benko in midfield, the Jones twins – real bread and butter players - you could always rely on them..."*

Mick Higgins
(Source: Lancashire Evening Telegraph)

Higgins recalls that goalkeeper Roberts made a great save in the very last minute of the final at Gigg Lane to salvage the replay. Then, in the rematch at the Anchor Ground, it was Higgins himself who scored the all important equalising goal: *"I can still picture it now: it was lashing down and I just managed to beat the offside trap. I let loose a shot from 25 yards out and it curled into the top corner"*

Although scoring the goal was special moment, Higgins was pleased for Jimmy Birkett; *"I remember seeing him in tears afterwards, pleased that he had finally won something. People like him deserve it"*.

Demise of a Winning Team

Even before that successful season, Jimmy Birkett had already decided to retire as first team manager, as he explains:

"I'd had a long time in football. I'd fulfilled my ambitions in a way by winning something and I could see people would come in for Malcolm Darling. He was never an outstanding player at Blackburn Rovers but he had an outstanding football brain. Harold Martin was another - he was on a par. I was going to go upstairs as General Manager and Malcolm Darling was coming in as manager with Harold as his assistant. It would have been a terrific set up if we could have kept that same team and built on it..."

According to Jimmy, during the close season, some of the more junior players at the club began rocking the boat and said that they would play for no money: *"...and the wage structure that had that kept the team together which had won the cup and finished 6th in the league - in a good league - was smashed. So Malcolm Darling said "well, if that's happening, I'm away...." and that was the decline of Darwen Football Club, unfortunately."*

"So I was back as caretaker manager for about 3 months. Then they went and made Steve Mullen manager - but he wasn't really manager material."

Mullen resigned as manager in November 1983 after the team had gone for four months without earning a single point. Club Chairman at the time, Dennis Jepson, said: *"Not only have we lost a manager, we have lost a good player who, on his day, had undoubted talent."*

Mullen went to play with Clitheroe and can still be seen playing today in the Darwen local leagues.

At the end of the 1983/84 season, Darwen finished bottom of Division 1 with only two wins and two draws from their 38 games. They were relegated to the Division 2 where they were to stay for three seasons.

1987 – The "Salmoners" Club

Back in the First Division for the 1987/88 season, the club was able to unveil the latest stage in its long rebuilding programme in the shape of a new 50-seater supporters' club bar at the ground. The addition of the bar had an immediate effect on attendances with some 200 people attending the first friendly game of the season.

The ground was further improved in 1987 when new floodlights were added at a cost of £10.000 and the team was given a new red and white strip sponsored by Ribble Buses, enabling them to return to their traditional "Arsenal-related" colours.

There followed a period of relative calm within the club as the team managed successive top ten finishes in the NWCFL , coming 6th, 7th 5th and 6th in the years from 1987 to 1990.

1990 – Lancashire Floodlit Trophy

Norman Walsh, a former director of Darwen Football Club, remembers that the original *Lancashire Floodlit Trophy* was a very good local level competition: *"but the whole thing was spoilt because the North West Counties League brought in their own floodlit trophy and it hit this one on the head. The biggest problem they had was fitting all the fixtures in. That's really how Darwen got to the final - they got a bye in the semi final as the other team couldn't get fixed up."*

Darwen entertained Stalybridge in the final at the Anchor Ground and were 3-0 down very early on, as Norman recalls: *"they were well in front and they led for a long time. Then in the second half we turned it round and beat them 4-3. It was a real cracking game!"*

July 1990 – Fire At Ground

Just as supporters of Darwen were beginning to look forward to the new season with optimism following the team's cup success, the club was hit by another setback. At the beginning of July, the clubhouse and changing rooms were completely destroyed by fire following an arson attack.

The Anchor Ground after the fire
(Source: Lancashire Evening Telegraph)

Mike Elsworth, who had, by then, taken over as chairman, said: *"The damage was absolutely horrendous. The cost of rebuilding the clubhouse and referee's room will be astronomical"*.

Club directors, officials, players and supporters all gave up their holidays in attempt to try and have the ground ready for the new season. The North West Counties League was also very supportive and allowed the club to retain its place in the league while remedial work was being carried out.

Jimmy Khan

Darwen's World Cup Star

Jimmy Khan was born in Darwen in September 1963 and, from a very young age, showed an aptitude for football. As a youth, he attracted interest from teams such as Manchester United and Tottenham Hotspur but decided to sign as a schoolboy for Blackburn Rovers.

For the next two years, he played with or against such players as Mark Hughes and Paul McGrath and was fully expected to be offered an apprenticeship when he turned 16.

Jimmy Khan
(Source: Darwen FC)

This did not work out, although he was offered the chance to stay as a non-contract player, meaning he could train and play but wouldn't get paid. He was invited for a trial at Bury but there again was only offered a non-contract arrangement but he reluctantly decided to accept and he played for Bury for two years, mostly in the youth team and occasionally in the reserves.

When he turned 18, Jimmy was told that Bury couldn't offer him a better deal so he left and ended up playing for a team in Finland during the summer months and with Darwen during the winter. His manager at the time, Jimmy Birkett, remembers him as *"a nice lad, young and enthusiastic - always keen to learn."*

Khan was the star of the team in Finland for two seasons but came back to England in 1984. Since then he has been able to combine playing with various NWCFL teams with working as a sports development officer for local authorities.

In 1987 he went to Rawalpindi, Pakistan, on a family visit and was talked into playing a couple of football games with some soldiers on the local army base. His goal scoring must have impressed one of the generals who was spectating as he was later invited back to play in Pakistan's qualification matches for the 1990 World Cup finals, which just coincided with another family trip to Rawalpindi.

Jimmy wasn't even planning to go on the trip but was on the plane like a shot once his father called to say he was wanted to play in an international trial: *"I couldn't come out quick enough. It didn't even enter my head that I could fail the trials and not even get to play. I was just so excited that I took the first plane out."*

But Jimmy went down with flu as soon as he arrived. The Pakistan coach couldn't risk taking him to the away qualifiers but asked him to stay for another month and get fit for the home game against the United Arab Emirates.

The game was played in the 80,000-seater Jinnah Stadium in Islamabad and ended in a 4-1 defeat for Pakistan but the game was understandably the biggest of Jimmy Khan's life, even if it was over too quickly for his liking: *"I can remember phases when I did something good but the match seemed to last only a few minutes before we were back in the dressing room again."*

After the match he was offered the chance to stay in Pakistan, but Jimmy refused: *"Although I played football for Pakistan, I saw myself as British. At the time, if Bobby Robson had called I would have played for him but he never rang. England was where I lived, it was where I was brought up. I had assumed English values and thought more than like an Englishman than a Pakistani."*

Jimmy Khan played football for several clubs in the NWCFL and, following Steve Wilkes' appointment as Darwen manager in 1997, he was tempted back to his home town club.

As well as his own sports development and coaching duties, he also works for the Football Association as an adviser on Asians in football and also teaches coaches how to coach.

The Steve Wilkes Era

Against the odds, Darwen managed to rebuild the ground once again and also keep their place in the NWCFL Division One, although they spent most of the 1990s looking over their shoulders at the relegation places rather than challenging for top honours.

A new chairman arrived in the shape of Kath Marah in 1994 and, despite having no money, the team continued to battle on.

Steve Wilkes
(Source: Darwen FC)

During the close season of 1997, manager Ian McGarry parted company with the club after some 10 years in charge of team affairs.
The man who stepped in to replace him was Steve Wilkes.

The Preston lad had started off as an apprentice at Wigan Athletic and then signed for Preston North End. After two years there, the Preston manager John McGrath told him that he was *"the best full back I've ever worked with but 6 inches too short..."*

Wilkes spent a year at Southport and was playing for Morecambe when he broke his femur in a car crash and was told he would never play football again. He proved the doctors wrong and, after 2½ years lay off, played for 3 seasons at Bamber Bridge.

Ian Mc Garry approached him to play for Darwen and a year later he became captain. When McGarry left, Wilkes was invited to take over.

He reveals that it was hard decision to make: *"I was only 29 at the time. It was a big decision, really, so I sought advice off people I knew."*

He was advised to give it a go and, in August 1997, became the new Darwen manager but he quickly discovered how hard it was to be the one in charge and to have to be the one to make those important decisions:

"When I did take over, I found it very, very difficult. It was strange a period for me personally as well – a bit of a learning curve really. We were getting beaten 6s and 7s and I didn't have any money to bring players in so I was relying on people that I knew. But then I learnt that you can't rely on people that are friends. If they're not good enough they're not good enough".

In the end, Wilkes realised that the club needed a complete rebuild in order to move forward.

"People like Phil Rose came in - he knew a few players - who helped me immensely. Paul Baker came along – he's been an absolute diamond for the club really, as well as the league's top goal scorer for the past 2 seasons. Neil Durkin came back to the club – was outstanding for 2 years – now he's playing for Leigh RMI in the Conference".

Season 1997/98

Steve Wilkes's first season in charge started badly with a 4-2 defeat away at Haslingden on the opening day of the season.

The team suffered injuries to key players early in the season and Wilkes himself was suspended for the first 9 weeks for having picked up 15 yellow cards as a player the previous season.

They lost 4 straight games in a row and were 3-0 up at home to Glossop but only managed to draw 3-3 and then got hammered 5-0 away at leaders Kidsgrove.

There was some consolation in the NWCFL Floodlit Trophy first round away at Clitheroe, which turned out to be a very bruising encounter. The home side finished the game with only 9 men through injuries as Darwen came away with a surprise 2-0 win.

The *Clitheroe Advertiser* described the match thus: *"Darwen are always a bruising and bustling side but on Monday night they surpassed themselves. Two Clitheroe players were carried off the field with ankle ligament damage and two others hobbled off at half time to take no further part in the game."*

Still in the middle of his ban, Wilkes could only stand by and watch as his team were hammered at home by 7 goals to 1 by Glossop in the NWCFL Challenge Cup. *"I have played football for 14 years and never felt so embarrassed as by this defeat,"* he said and promised to make sweeping changes.

The return Floodlit trophy game with Clitheroe turned out to be another disappointment for the Darwen side as their 2 goal first leg advantage was wiped out and Clitheroe won the tie 3-2 overall.

By mid November, Darwen were bottom of the NWCFL Division One table with just a single win and two draws to show from their 16 league games. During that time Steve Wilkes had been forced to use 44 players through injuries and suspensions - including an amazing 7 goalkeepers.

Wilkes himself was back in the fray for the visit of Rossendale and saw his team once again surrender a 2-goal lead before getting himself sent off again towards the end of the 3-5 defeat.

On 6th December, two sensational goals by centre forward Ian Latham gave Darwen their first league point for over a month with a 2-2 draw at St Helens Town. But the improvement was short lived and three defeats on the trot followed.

The club was given a new year boost by the quick return of Denny Khan who had moved to Haslingden a few weeks before and a 0-0 draw away at Warrington was followed up by a much needed win 1-

0 at home to Salford, Khan's 35th minute goal securing the Reds' first win in the league in 22 games – dating back to August.

Buoyed by three clean sheets in three games, Steve Wilkes set his team the task of winning 5 of their remaining 7 games in order to stay up in the First Division.

But all too often the luck in front of goal was not there. Darwen found themselves having to make do with draws instead of wins and losing to single goal defeats that should have been draws.

At a crucial time of the season, Denny Khan picked up a thigh strain and missed key games. Darwen signed Paul Baker from Clitheroe as a last ditch attempt to get the goals needed to fight relegation.

In mid-March Darwen finally put a mini run of results together, with 3 draws (away at Vauxhall Motors, home to Chadderton and home to Haslingden) and a win (home to Nantwich, 2-0) giving them enough points to move off the bottom of the table for the first time since early November.

That form continued into April with a draw at Mossley and a win at home to third from bottom Atherton Collieries but any hopes of salvation were shattered the next day with a 5-1 hammering at Glossop.

With influential player Matt Atkinson out for the rest of the season with a burst appendix, Darwen slipped back to the bottom of the table on goal difference after a 4-1 defeat at Nantwich.

A 3-1 win over Clitheroe on 2nd May gave Darwen a slim mathematical hope of staying up, but the North West Counties Football League had already sealed the club's fate at a meeting of their ground grading committee. Even if they managed to get enough points to stay out of the two relegation places at the end of the season, Darwen would be relegated anyway.

The Committee announced that Darwen, Chadderton and Warrington Town would all be relegated from the First Division for failing to complete work on facilities for the 1st April deadline.

In Darwen's case, this work included building a new referee's room, adding a second toilet block and concreting behind one goal, as a hard standing area 1metre wide was required all around the ground.

The club had been plagued by vandalism all season and Club Chairman Kath Marah was angered by the decision: *"if you look at our ground compared to others, it is certainly not the worst."*

Kath Marah
(Source: Lancashire Evening Telegraph)

" We only found out at the end of October what needed doing but, when you can only get money in through the gate it is very difficult. They ask us to do these jobs and have them completed by the end of March when the football season is at its busiest. Why can't they put a deadline on the job like the end of June?"

"Vandalism is costing us several thousand pounds a year in damages and that is money we could have devoted to improving the state of the ground."

Darwen's last game of the season was another one to forget. They lost 5-0 at home to Kidsgrove, having Lyndon Howarth and Neil Cordingley sent off.

Season 1998/99

Darwen's centenary season at the Anchor Ground kicked off more or less in the same way as the previous century had finished - with a visit by a Manchester United XI. Quite fitting as Darwen FC's last match in the Football League in the 1898/99 season had been at home to Newton Heath – forerunner of the modern day Red Devils.

Darwen v Man Utd XI
(Source: Lancashire Evening Telegraph)

A good 500 crowd was treated to an entertaining evening as the Old Trafford side, fielding such stars of the future as Luke Chadwick, George Clegg and Lee Roche, raced to an easy 3-0 half time lead. It was 6-0 twenty minutes later and then Darwen forward Dave Atkinson received the biggest cheer of the night with his 75th minute goal to make the final score Darwen 1 Man Utd 6.

Behind the scenes, fans, club officials and players alike had been working hard to complete the necessary ground improvements in the run up to the new season. Local firms had helped by donating building materials but the work was made harder by continual attacks by vandals breaking things and scrawling graffiti.

The first game down in Division 2 went like a dream as Darwen won 3-1 away at Tetley Walker on Monday 17th August but they were brought back down to earth with a bump two days later with a 5-1 defeat at Squires Gate.

The first home game of the season turned out to be a bruising encounter against Formby, and Darwen were under pressure from the start, losing 3-1. They picked themselves up from that setback and embarked on a 5 game unbeaten run - winning 3 and drawing 2 - despite missing 9 first team players through injury.

That run came to an end away at Bacup on 12th September when 9 men lost 2-1 and insult was added to injury when, a week later, the reds were unceremoniously dumped out of the FA Cup by Billingham Synthonia by an embarrassing 7-0 scoreline.

Darwen remained in close contention for a promotion spot for much of the season and put together an impressive 12 match unbeaten run that extended to the end of January, when goalkeeper Lee Purvis won the Second Division safe hands award for keeping a clean sheet in all but one of his games.

However, it was the ATS Trophy - the new sponsored name for the Lancashire Junior Cup - that was to be their best chance of success as the season wore on. They won 3-0 away at Atherton LR in the first round and 2-0 away at Nelson in the second and the draw for the quarter final brought local rivals Accrington Stanley to the Anchor Ground for what Steve Wilkes billed as the club's *"biggest match in years"*.

The game on 2nd February started badly for Darwen as Accrington took a 2 goal lead in the first 5 minutes but Darwen dug deep and, with a large vocal support, equalised by half time through goals from Whittaker and Curley. The match remained on a knife edge as Accrington put on the pressure for much of the second half. In the dying seconds, Steve Lynch flicked on Neil Durkin's free kick and Whittaker unleashed a fierce 25 yard volley which smashed into the roof of the net for a last minute winner.

They were drawn against Southport in the semi final – a tie that pleased Steve Wilkes: *"it's a great tie for me because I played there for 12 months and had a brilliant time."*

157

Unfortunately, the cup run began to get in the way of the league campaign as many players' minds were already on the semi final and the promotion push began to lose momentum with points dropped at Castleton, Curzon Aston and Warrington

Steve Wilkes said: *"the lads haven't really been the same since we beat Accrington. So it has obviously affected them. I don't think we could catch Fleetwood now but if we can finish in the top four we could still go up because some of the other clubs' grounds might not be up to it."*

As Darwen approached their semi final at Southport, the manager was in confident mood: *"nobody would have given us a chance of getting this far so why shouldn't we go all the way?"*

The Sandgrounders had won the trophy the previous season and were obviously taking Darwen as a serious threat. Despite making changes from the team that had played in the Conference the previous weekend, their line up for the game on Monday 15th March included many first team players – notably former England semi-pro international Brian Ross and £16,000 signing Lee Trundle.

But things did not go quite according to plan and the form book was turned on its head when Paul Baker scored for the underdogs with a fierce 16 yard shot after just 9 minutes. He repeated the trick some 25 minutes later when gifted a chance by a mix up in the Southport defence and, with Lee Trundle sent off before half time for two bookable offences, it looked as if Darwen were in for a good night.

After 60 minutes, it was 3-0 to Darwen as Michael Douglas finished off a great move set up by Steve Wilkes and Mick Lynch and, four minutes from time, added his second and Darwen's fourth from the penalty spot.

Wilkes, who made a big impact after coming on a substitute in the 48th minute, was elated at the result: *"I cannot wait to get back to Deepdale. All my players are up for it. It was important to keep a clean sheet early on. Paul Baker scored an excellent first goal that set us up."*

However, as the date of the final approached, the Lancashire FA dropped a bombshell. The venue for the match was to be switched to Chorley's Victory Park as Preston North End wanted to protect their pitch in case they reached the League play offs.

Steve Wilkes - who had been looking forward to going back to the home of one of his first clubs - was angered by the decision and thought that the LFA should have at least moved the match to another Football League ground – such as Blackburn or Bolton: *"this is a prestigious competition which has been going since 1885 and I think they've made a mockery of it.*

"We are at the bottom of the non-league pyramid and there is no team lower than us in status who can get to the final of this competition. I think the players should be rewarded for getting us there."

Darwen's ATS Trophy Final Team
Back: Bright, Curley, Elmer, Atkinson, Purvis, Lynch, Wilkes
Front: Durkin, Rose, Khan, Almond, Baker, Cordingley, Douglas
<small>(Source: Darwen FC)</small>

13th April 1999 – ATS Trophy Final

Darwen hadn't won the Lancashire Junior Cup since 1933 and had not even reached the final since 1949 while their opponents Morecambe, of the Conference, had appeared in the previous three finals.

Undeterred by the 4 leagues' difference between the two clubs, manager Steve Wilkes was in fighting spirit: *"No-one gave us a chance against Accrington but we beat them after being 2-0 down and certainly no-one expected us to win at Southport and we stuffed them 4-0".*

The game itself was a joy to watch and, for the most part, it was very difficult to tell which of the two sides was the Conference team, despite Morecambe having ex Blackpool goalkeeper Steve McIlhargey, ex Preston Northender Andy Fensome and the Confernce's top goal scorer John Norman in their ranks.

The large, vocal Morecambe contingent in the crowd was stunned into silence on 39 minutes when Darwen took a surprise lead. Paul Baker swung in a cross from the left that which Neil Almond gleefully headed into the bottom corner of the net.

Neil Almond celebrates Darwen's first goal
(Source: Lancashire Evening Telegraph)

160

But before the underdogs even had time to celebrate, Morecambe equalised just 30 seconds from the restart with a breakaway that split the Darwen defence.

The game continued at a breathtaking pace and just two minutes later Darwen took the lead again after Michael Douglas (grandson of former Blackburn Rovers and England winger Bryan Douglas) latched onto another Baker cross to fire home Darwen's second goal of the game.

Michael Douglas puts Darwen back into the lead
(Source: Lancashire Evening Telegraph)

This time, they held onto the lead and went into the dressing room at half time with a 2-1 advantage over their high flying rivals.

In the second half, Morecambe brought more pressure to bear and finally equalised with 18 minutes left to play. The score remained level at full time and Darwen held the Conference side for a further 30 minutes of extra time and took the tie to penalties.

Morecambe missed their first kick but Douglas and Durkin both missed for Darwen and Morecambe went on to win the penalty shoot out 4-2.

Speaking recently about the final, Steve Wilkes said that it has been the highlight so far of his managerial career: *"Just being 18 minutes away from beating a first team side of Morecambe's stature."*

"The thing that stood out for me that day was when it went to extra time and I asked my players who wants to take a penalty and seven or eight hands went up without hesitation.

I work with Andy Fensome, who was playing for Morecambe, and the told me later said that when Jim Harvey asked the Morecambe players, only two put their hands up – and they were on something like £200 a week...! It was outstanding from my lads."

Once the cup final was over, it was time to return to back to more mundane matters such as the league campaign but Darwen finished on a low ebb, losing their last home games of the season 0-1 to Fleetwood and 2-3 to Abbey Hey.

Season 1999/2000

In the run up to the new season, Steve Wilkes announced that he would be staying at Darwen, despite having been approached by "*a leading Unibond League club*" following the successful cup run.

During the summer he was able to strengthen the side by signing Scott Derbyshire from Ramsbottom and getting Denny Khan back from Bacup.

The season started well as Darwen won their first two league games, beating Tetley Walker 5-0 and Colne 1-0 but then history repeated itself with another FA Cup defeat - this time 1-0 - at home to Billingham.

Following that, the Darreners embarked on an 7 game unbeaten run, the only point being dropped in a 0-0 draw home draw with Nelson, who had also made an unbeaten start to the league season.

In October they put another winning run together and, after a 4-1 victory over Chadderton on a cold Friday night, Darwen were top of the league table. Paul Baker scored his 22nd goal of the season in that game and the team then remained unbeaten in the league until Boxing Day when they went down 3-0 at home to Bacup.

Lee Purvis
(Source: Darwen FC)

Lee Purvis made his 100th consecutive appearance in goal for Darwen during that period but a 1-0 defeat away at Curzon Ashton in a top of the table clash in mid January left the club losing ground in their bid for promotion

Darwen were drawn away at First Division Great Harwood in the Marsden Trophy (Lancashire Junior Cup) and came away with a 3-1 extra time victory after having dominated most of the match.

That win handed them a plum home tie against Unibond Premier League high flyers Marine, which they lost by the narrowest of single goal margins 1-0.

The reds also received a home draw in the North West Counties Floodlit Trophy and they took First Division side Kidsgrove to a replay having drawn 1-1 at the Anchor after extra time. The replay ended in a 3-1 defeat and meant that Darwen could, once again, concentrate on the league.

With 10 games left to go, Steve Wilkes set his team the target of 7 points from their next 3 games to keep in contention at the top of the table. Unfortunately a 4-1 defeat away at fellow promotion contenders Nelson and a 1-1 draw at home to Curzon Ashton left his team off target, despite a 2-1 win at Squires Gate in between.

One team that had been quietly closing in on the promotion hunt was Woodley Sports who, unfortunately, had been Darwen's bogey team throughout the season. They had already lost to them at home in the league cup and then managed to repeat the feat in the league as well, dropping some more important promotion points, causing Wilkes to comment: *"We have not beaten anyone in the top five and that is what has kept us down"*.

A single goal defeat at Chadderton prompted Wilkes to make a bold approach to Blackburn Rovers' Franz Carr, who he knew from his days with Preston schoolboys. The former Nottingham Forest winger was out of favour at Ewood Park at the time but, unfortunately for Darwen, did not fancy dropping down to such a level.

A 5-1 win away at Bacup looked to be the springboard for a final promotion push but a bad tempered 3-1 defeat at home to Warrington, with 2 Darwen players sent off and a further 8 bookings, handed the initiative back to Nelson for the second promotion place

The 2-0 defeat away at Alsager at the end of April which Wilkes described as *"awful"* mean that the Anchormen finished the season in fourth place and could only watch as Woodley Sports won their games in hand to leapfrog themselves and Nelson into second place.

The only consolation after a hard fought season was that Paul Baker ended up the league's top scorer with 25 league and 5 cup goals.

Season 2000/01

The 2000/01 season was a disappointing one for fans and players alike as, after the previous season's promotion push, hopes were high for a top two finish this time around.

In many ways the team's fortunes mirrored those of the previous season. Up to Christmas they were very much in contention but bad weather marred much of the campaign and Darwen had trouble getting games staged.

After the Christmas period, Darwen had several games in hand over the top clubs and might have caught them but being forced to play so many of their home games on cold winter nights in driving wind and rain took much of the shine off their play.

Several such fixtures in a row produced back to back home defeats - notably against Tetley Walker and Alsager - and the team was left looking at nothing better than a mid table finish.

One high point was the first round of the League Cup, where they beat First Division Prescot Cables 3-2 in a thrilling game but did not progress past the next round, coming unstuck away at Squires Gate.

Steve Wilkes decided that it was time to start building for the future and used the last few games of the season to try out some new young players. Although this resulted in several defeats, there were also some memorable end of season home games against Holker Old Boys (7-0 win), Bootle (5-3) and Formby (3-1) to round off the season with a bit of a cheer.

Paul Baker's 2 goals in final home game of the season against Formby were just enough for him to be crowned the Second Division's top goal scorer for the second season running.

Matt Atkinson

Matt Atkinson has been a player at Darwen for over 15 years and he and his wife Lynn both work tirelessly behind the scenes for the benefit of the club.

Matt Atkinson
(Source: Darwen FC)

Lynn is, officially speaking, the club's fixture secretary but she is just as likely to be found working behind the bar in the club house, on the refreshment counter or even on the gate on a matchday, such is the enthusiasm and dedication of all the behind-the-scenes helpers at Darwen Football Club.

Matt Atkinson is *"Mr Darwen"* and Steve Wilkes is full of praise for his assistant: *"Outstanding – you can't run a football club like Darwen without people like that. I couldn't have done the job without him."*

Matt doesn't just concentrate on team affairs either, he also looks after the pitch: *"Many a time we've turned up at quarter to two for a game and he's been marking out the pitch. I've started my team talk at 2 o'clock and he's still there marking the lines out or something..."*

Steve says that Matt is still playing well after 15 years in the team but *"he doesn't play enough because he keeps getting sent off. But that shows he's committed to he cause – referees know him now, which is unfair. If you or I did something we'd get a talking to, if Matt does it he gets a yellow card for it."*

Looking To The Future

Always with an eye on improvement, Steve Wilkes is trying to make Darwen as professional as possible: *"when I took over I made every one wear shirts and ties, be there at a certain time, wear clean boots, club tracksuits. It gives the players a greater feeling of pride."*

He has appointed Jimmy Khan as first team coach, although he still sees him as a key player in the team as well, but *"unfortunately for Jimmy, he's been injured more than Matt's been sent off"*.

Khan has his FA coaching badge and does a lot of work for the FA. At the bottom end of the football pyramid, networking is important. He has already introduced several new young players to the club and Steve Wilkes feels that sort of contact is vitally important for bringing new talent to the club:

"If I go and watch a player and the first thing they ask is how much are you going to offer me. My answer is nothing they'll often as not say they rather play in the West Lancs League for 20 quid."

Looking ahead, Mr Wilkes is not planning on hanging up his own playing boots just yet, despite having niggling knee problems as a result of his car accident:

"I don't think it'll stop me playing – it's in my blood. I might give it one last year and then concentrate on management."

The End
(of the beginning....)

DARWEN FC COMPLETE LEAGUE RECORD
1889-2001

Football Alliance

SEASON	LEAGUE	P	W	D	L	F	A	P	POS
1889-90	Alliance	22	10	2	10	70	75	22	6/12
1890-91	Alliance	22	10	3	9	64	59	23	6/12

Football League

SEASON		P	W	D	L	F	A	PT	POS
1891-92	F/L	26	4	3	19	38	112	11	14/14
1892-93	Div 2	22	14	2	6	60	36	30	3/12
1893-94	Div 1	30	7	5	18	37	83	19	15/16
1894-95	Div 2	30	16	4	10	74	43	36	6/16
1895-96	Div2	30	12	6	12	72	67	30	9/16
1896-97	Div 2	30	14	0	16	67	61	28	11/16
1897-98	Div 2	30	6	2	22	31	76	14	15/16
1898-99	Div 2	34	2	5	27	22	141	9	18/18

Lancashire League

SEASON		P	W	D	L	F	A	PT	POS
1899-00	LANCS	28	13	10	5	56	31	36	5/15
1900-01	LANCS	20	10	3	7	40	25	23	4/11
1901-02	LANCS	24	18	6	0	78	16	42	1/13
1902-03	LANCS	22	15	1	6	68	21	31	2/12

Lancashire Combination

SEASON	DIV	P	W	D	L	F	A	Pt	POS
1903-04	LAN C-1	34	19	7	8	79	45	45	5/18
1904-05	LAN C-1	34	14	10	10	55	49	38	5/18
1905-06	LAN C-1	38	19	9	10	81	64	47	2/20
1906-07	LAN C-1	38	17	8	13	60	55	42	7/20
1907-08	LAN C-1	38	11	8	19	52	85	30	16/20
1908-09	LAN C-1	38	13	5	20	41	85	31	17/20
1909-10	LAN C-2	38	15	6	17	71	68	36	11/20
1910-11	LAN C-2	38	13	3	22	59	91	29	1720
1911-12	LAN C-2	30	9	3	18	34	84	21	13/16
1912-13	LAN C-2	34	9	5	20	53	85	23	14/18
1913-14	LAN C-2	34	15	6	13	66	65	36	8/18
1914-20		No participation due to World War 1							

Lancashire Combination - InterWar Years

SEASON	DIV	P	W	D	L	F	A	PT	POS
1920-21	LAN C-1	34	17	10	7	79	51	44	4/18
1921-22	LAN C-1	34	21	3	10	75	51	45	4/18
1922-23	LAN C-1	34	17	9	8	77	60	43	3/18
1923-24	LAN C-1	38	19	8	11	84	63	46	3/20
1924-25	LAN C-1	38	17	11	8	64	35	45	3/20
1925-26	LAN C-1	38	18	4	16	93	75	40	9/20
1926-27	LAN C-1	38	15	6	17	89	98	36	12/20
1927-28	LAN C-1	38	10	6	22	68	104	26	19/20
1928-29	LAN C-1	38	17	5	16	84	82	39	11/20
1929-30	LAN C-1	38	22	4	12	93	68	48	4/20
1930-31	LAN C-1	38	28	7	8	116	55	53	1/20
1931-32	LAN C-1	36	24	7	5	104	43	55	1/19
1932-33	LAN C-1	38	22	5	11	119	67	49	4/20
1933-34	LAN C-1	38	20	7	11	122	72	47	5/20
1934-35	LAN C-1	38	19	6	13	119	83	44	6/20
1935-36	LAN C-1	40	21	3	16	104	77	45	8/20
1936-37	LAN C-1	40	24	7	9	106	63	55	3/21
1937-38	LAN C-1	42	19	9	14	103	85	47	7/22
1938-39	LAN C-1	42	18	6	18	116	87	42	13/22
1939-45			No	participation	due	to	World	War 2		

Lancashire Combination - Post War Competition

SEASON	LEAGUE	P	W	D	L	F	A	P	POS
1945-46	LAN C-1	22	9	7	6	50	48	25	5/12
1946-47	LAN C-1	42	14	6	22	84	122	34	18/22
1947-48	LAN C-1	42	12	9	21	60	91	33	16/22
1948-49	LAN C-1	42	21	7	14	81	65	49	5/22
1949-50	LAN C-1	42	13	11	18	55	66	37	17/20
1950-51	LAN C-1	42	12	12	18	62	79	36	15/22
1951-52	LAN C-1	42	16	5	21	60	83	37	16/22
1952-53	LAN C-1	42	19	11	12	88	65	49	3/22
1953-54	LAN C-1	40	18	9	13	80	49	45	5/21
1954-55	LAN C-1	42	15	13	14	64	79	43	12/22
1955-56	LAN C-1	38	13	8	17	66	85	44	13/20
1956-57	LAN C-1	38	11	5	22	62	88	27	19/20
1957-58	LAN C-1	42	14	6	22	71	104	34	18/22
1958-59	LAN C-1	42	16	6	20	75	93	38	14/22
1959-60	LAN C-1	42	10	11	21	57	86	31	20/22
1960-61	LAN C-1	42	7	2	33	45	121	16	22/22
1961-62	LAN C-1	42	8	9	25	56	119	25	19/22
1962-63	LAN C-1	42	5	6	31	41	117	16	21/22
1963-64	LAN C-2	34	14	10	10	77	59	38	9/18
1964-65	LAN C-2	32	15	12	5	63	58	35	11/17
1965-66	LAN C-2	26	15	9	2	52	33	32	3/14
1966-67	LAN C-1	42	6	12	24	56	102	24	21/22

Lancashire Combination cont'd

SEASON	DIV	P	W	D	L	F	A	PT	POS
1967-68	LAN C-2	32	21	6	5	72	55	48	2/17
1968-69	LAN C-1	42	17	9	16	59	64	43	8/22
1969/70	LAN C-1	38	15	11	12	78	67	41	10/20
1970/71	LAN C-1	30	10	6	14	44	57	26	11/16
1971/72	LAN C-1	28	10	6	12	48	57	26	9/15
1972/73	LAN C-1	38	30	4	4	105	39	64	1/20
1973/74	LAN C-1	38	24	10	4	89	38	58	2/20
1974/75	LAN C-1	38	26	8	4	97	36	60	1/20

Cheshire County League

SEASON	DIV	P	W	D	L	F	A	PT	POS
1975-76	CHES	42	9	7	26	49	89	25	20/22
1976-77	CHES	42	10	8	24	50	81	28	19/22
1977-78	CHES	42	14	6	22	50	68	34	15/22
1978-79	CHES-1	42	15	9	18	52	53	39	15/22
1979-80	CHES-1	38	12	12	14	41	52	36	10/20
1980-81	CHES-1	38	8	10	20	46	74	26	17/20
1981-82	CHES-1	38	16	10	12	63	62	40	7/20

North West Counties League

SEASON	DIV	P	W	D	L	F	A	PT	POS
1982-83	NWC-1	38	17	12	9	68	46	46	6/20
1983-84	NWC-1	38	2	2	34	29	111	6	20/20
1984-85	NWC-2	34	7	6	21	32	62	20	16/18
1985-86	NWC-2	34	8	8	18	48	57	24	15/18
1986-87	NWC-2	34	15	8	11	45	47	38	6/18
1987-88	NWC-1	34	14	10	10	55	45	38	7/18
1988-89	NWC-1	34	19	9	6	64	36	47	5/18
1989-90	NWC-1	34	15	9	10	40	34	54	6/18
1990-91	NWC-1	36	9	11	16	44	62	38	16/19
1991-92	NWC-1	34	10	11	13	56	55	41	10/18
1992-93	NWC-1	42	14	10	18	54	61	52	17/22
1993-94	NWC-1	42	12	8	22	38	61	44	16/22
1994-95	NWC-1	42	14	5	23	65	82	47	17/22
1995-96	NWC-1	42	9	10	23	57	77	37	19/22
1996-97	NWC-1	42	9	10	23	49	82	37	21/22
1997-98	NWC-1	42	6	13	23	42	93	31	21/22
1998-99	NWC-2	36	13	12	11	64	53	51	8/19
1999-00	NWC-2	34	20	6	8	69	35	66	4/18
2000-01	NWC-2	38	16	7	15	72	66	55	11/20

You've read the book.
Now visit the club!

Darwen Football Club
Anchor Ground, Anchor Road,
Darwen BB3 0BB
Telephone (01254) 705627

Directions to the Anchor Ground:

- o *Take the M65 towards Blackburn*
- o *Exit at Junction 4 (also signposted for Ewood Park)*
- o *Turn left at traffic lights, head towards Darwen*
- o *Go straight over mini roundabout*
- o *Turn left between Anchor Garage and Anchor Pub*
- o *Fork right alongside Anchor Estate*
- o *Anchor Ground is at bottom of road*
- o *Ample car parking adjacent to ground*

Note: We are already collecting material for a second volume of Darwen FC memories. If **you** have any photos, newspaper cuttings, programmes, memorabilia or just good memories as a player or supporter, please contact the club.

About The Author

Paul Breeze worked for 10 years as a senior contracts controller and in-house translator for an international manufacturing company. He speaks fluent French and German and studied a BA (Hons) degree in Journalism and Languages at the University of Central Lancashire in Preston

He is a former Sports Editor for Radio Europe 2, Luxembourg and is currently working as a freelance translator and sports journalist, with notable media involvement in:

- 1996 European Football Championships
- 1997 World Table Tennis Championships
- 1998 European Junior Ice Hockey Championships
- 1999 Cricket World Cup

He has recently taken over as Editor of "Elfmeter", the quarterly English language magazine about German football, and is also working on several other projects.

Other books by the same author:
- *The BBC & Radio Luxembourg*
- *The History of FC Rot Weiss Erfurt - Forgotten Champions of DDR Football*
- *The History of DDR Football from 1945 to 2000*
- *20 years of the Peterborough Pirates - A Fans' Eye View*

For more details, please send an SAE to:
Posh Up North Publishing, 3 Hunter Street, Nelson, Lancs BB9 5JG